M

ing
n

A

THE FLASH OF LIGHTNING BEHIND THE MOUNTAIN

also by **CHARLES BUKOWSKI**

Available From ＥＣＣＯ

The Days Run Away Like Wild Horses Over the Hills *(1969)*

Post Office *(1971)*

Mockingbird Wish Me Luck *(1972)*

South of No North *(1973)*

Burning in Water, Drowning in Flame: Selected Poems 1955–1973 *(1974)*

Factotum *(1975)*

Love Is a Dog from Hell: Poems 1974–1977 *(1977)*

Women *(1978)*

You Kissed Lilly *(1978)*

Play the Piano drunk Like a percussion instrument Until the fingers begin
   to bleed a bit *(1979)*

Shakespeare Never Did This *(1979)*

Dangling in the Tournefortia *(1981)*

Ham on Rye *(1982)*

Bring Me Your Love *(1983)*

Hot Water Music *(1983)*

There's No Business *(1984)*

War All the Time: Poems 1981–1984 *(1984)*

You Get So Alone at Times That It Just Makes Sense *(1986)*

The Movie: "Barfly" *(1987)*

The Roominghouse Madrigals: Early Selected Poems 1946–1966 *(1988)*

Hollywood *(1989)*

Septuagenarian Stew: Stories & Poems *(1990)*

The Last Night of the Earth Poems *(1992)*

Screams from the Balcony: Selected Letters 1960–1970 (Volume 1) *(1993)*

Pulp *(1994)*

Living on Luck: Selected Letters 1960s–1970s (Volume 2) *(1995)*

Betting on the Muse: Poems & Stories *(1996)*

Bone Palace Ballet: New Poems *(1997)*

The Captain Is Out to Lunch and the Sailors Have Taken Over the Ship *(1998)*

Reach for the Sun: Selected Letters 1978–1994 (Volume 3) *(1999)*

What Matters Most Is How Well You Walk Through the Fire: New Poems *(1999)*

Open All Night: New Poems *(2000)*

The Night Torn Mad with Footsteps: New Poems *(2001)*

Beerspit Night and Cursing: The Correspondence of Charles Bukowski &
   Sheri Martinelli 1960–1967 *(2001)*

Sifting through the madness for the Word, the line, the way: New Poems *(2003)*

Charles Bukowski

THE FLASH OF LIGHTNING BEHIND THE MOUNTAIN

new poems

Edited by John Martin

An Imprint of HarperCollinsPublishers

HarperCollins books may be purchased for educational, business, or sales promotional use. For information please write: Special Markets Department, HarperCollins Publishers, Inc., 10 East 53rd Street, New York, NY 10022.

These poems are part of an archive of unpublished work that Charles Bukowski left to be published after his death.

Grateful acknowledgement is made to John Martin, who edited these poems.

FIRST EDITION

Designed by Fearn Cutler de Vicq

Library of Congress Cataloging-in-Publication Data has been applied for.

ISBN 0-06-057701-0

04 05 06 07 08 BVG/QF 10 9 8 7 6 5 4 3 2 1

Contents

part 3.

THE FLASH OF
LIGHTNING BEHIND THE
MOUNTAIN

part 1.

I watch the old ladies
in the supermarket,
angry and alone.

German

being the German kid in the 20's in Los Angeles
was difficult.
there was much anti-German feeling then,
a carry-over from World War I.
gangs of kids chased me through the neighborhood
yelling, "Hienie! Hienie! Hienie!"
they never caught me.
I was like a cat.
I knew all the paths through brush and alleys.
I scaled 6-foot back fences in a flash and was off through
backyards and around blocks
and onto garage roofs and other hiding places.
then too, they didn't really want to catch me.
they were afraid I might bayonet them
or gouge out their eyes.

this went on for about 18 months
then all of a sudden it seemed to stop.
I was more or less accepted (but never really)
which was all right with me.
those sons-of-bitches were Americans,
they and their parents had been born here.
they had names like Jones and Sullivan and
Baker.
they were pale and often fat with runny
noses and big belt buckles.
I decided never to become an American.
my hero was Baron Manfred von Richthofen
the German air ace;
he'd shot down 80 of their best
and there was nothing they could do about
that now.
their parents didn't like my parents

(I didn't either) and
I decided when I got big I'd go live in some place
like Iceland,
never open my door to anybody and live on my
luck, live with a beautiful wife and a bunch of wild
animals:
which is, more or less, what
happened.

the old girl

she was very thin, gray, bent, and each day she
waited at the door of the
First Interstate Bank in San Pedro,
and as the people came and went she
approached them
one by one
and asked for money.

about 75% of the time
I respond to those who ask but with
the other 25% I am instinctively put off
and just don't have the will to
give.

the frail old woman at the bank put me off, she had
put me off for some time and we had a silent
understanding: I would lift my hand in a
gesture of protest and she would turn quickly
away. this had happened so often
that now she remembers and doesn't
approach me.

one noon I sat in my car and watched
her
and after 20 attempts she scored
17 times.

I drove off as she was approaching yet another
soft touch, and even so I
suddenly felt real guilt for my unfeeling habit of
refusing the old
girl.

later in the clubhouse at Hollywood
park

between the 6th and 7th races
I saw her again as she was going up the
aisle
frail and bent, a large wad of
paper money clutched tight in a bony hand
clearly on her way to
bet the next race.

of course, she had every right to
be there,
to place her bets with the rest of us,
she only wanted and needed
what most people want and need:
a chance.

I watched as she
reached the top of the aisle and
I saw her stop and speak to a young man
who smiled and then
handed her a
bill.

not to be distracted I
rose and went to the betting window
to place my own
wager.

and, going back to my seat
as I was
walking down the aisle she was
coming up and we saw one another
and without thinking
I held my hand up,

gently, in that familiar
gesture
she'd seen so often
in front of the bank.

she looked at me with
unblinking blue eyes and said,
"fuck you!"
as we passed on the stairs.

she was right, of course, it's
a matter of survival—General Motors does
it, you do it, the cat does it, so
does the bird, nations do it,
families do it, I do it,
the boxer sometimes does it,
it's done when you
buy a loaf of bread, it's done sometimes
out of madness and fear, it's
done in the doctor's office and
in the back alley,
it's done everywhere
all the time
over and over again:
we all want to survive.

it is the inevitable way
the familiar way
the way things
work.

I went back to my seat to
ponder all that but I

couldn't come up with anything useful at
all . . .

as the horses broke from the
gate
hustled by the crouching jocks
in their silks—
orange, blue, yellow, shocking pink,
green, chartreuse, a
stampeding rainbow of controlled
fury,
the sun shot through the
screaming
and I suddenly knew that
we are all caught forever in the
self-same trap
and I instantly forgave that old
girl
for belonging.

the birds

the acute and terrible air hangs with murder
as summer birds mingle in the branches
and warble
and mystify the clamour of the mind;
an old parrot
who never talks,
sits thinking in a Chinese laundry,
disgruntled
forsaken
celibate;
there is red on his wing
where there should be green,
and between us
the recognition of
an immense and wasted life.

. . . my 2nd wife left me
because I set our birds free:
one yellow, with crippled wing
quickly going down and to the left,
cat-meat,
cackling like an organ;
and the other,
mean green,
of empty thimble head,
popping up like a rocket
high into the hollow sky,
disappearing like sour love
and yesterday's desire
and leaving me
forever.

and when my wife
returned that night

with her bags and plans,
her tricks and shining greeds,
she found me
glittering over a yellow feather
seeking out the music
which she,
oddly,
failed to
hear.

game day

this lady was always after me about this or
that:
"what are those scratches on your back?"
"baby, I dunno, you must have put them
there."
"you've been with some whore!"

"what's that bite mark on your neck?
she must have been a *hot* number!"
"huh? baby, I don't see anything."
"there! there! on the left side of your
neck!
you musta really turned her on!"

"what's this phone number written inside this
matchbook?"
"what phone number?"
"this phone number! it's a woman's hand-
writing!"
"damned if I know where that came from."
"I'm going to call that number, that's what
I'll do!"
"go ahead."
"no, I'm going to tear it up, I'm going to tear
up that whore's number!"

"you made love to that neighbor woman in our bed
while I was at work!"
"what?"
"another neighbor told me! I was told she came
right into this house!"
"oh, that. she came by to borrow a cup of
sugar."

"a cup of sugar, my ass! you screwed her
right in this house, right in our bed with the
dog watching!"
"she just wanted a cup of sugar, she wasn't
here but two minutes!"
"a quicky! you gave her a quicky!"

later I found out she had screwed a guy in
the back of his delivery truck
and she had screwed an appliance salesman
in the crapper in the mens' room,
in a stall for the handicapped.
and there was something or other with a
meter reader, a blow job, I think.

she had completely outfoxed me with her
smoke screen of accusations
while she had been unfaithful on almost a
full-time basis.
and when confronted, her answer
was a "SO WHAT?"

I moved her out.
we flipped for the dog and she won.
and the next time the neighbor lady
came by to borrow a cup of sugar
she stayed longer than a minute or
two.

gas

my grandmother had a serious gas
problem.
we only saw her on Sunday.
she'd sit down to dinner
and she'd have gas.
she was very heavy,
80 years old.
wore this large glass brooch,
that's what you noticed most
in addition to the gas.
she'd let it go just as food was being served.
she'd let it go loud in bursts
spaced about a minute apart.
she'd let it go
4 or 5 times
as we reached for the potatoes
poured the gravy
cut into the meat.

nobody ever said anything,
especially me.
I was 6 years old.
only my grandmother spoke.
after 4 or 5 blasts
she would say in an offhand way,
"I will bury you all!"

I didn't much like that:
first farting
then saying that.

it happened every Sunday.
she was my father's mother.

every Sunday it was death and gas
and mashed potatoes and gravy
and that big glass brooch.

those Sunday dinners would
always end with apple pie and
ice cream
and a big argument
about something or other,
my grandmother finally running out the door
and taking the red train back to
Pasadena
the place stinking for an hour
and my father walking about
fanning a newspaper in the air and
saying, "it's all that damned sauerkraut
she eats!"

mystery leg

first of all, I had a hard time, a very hard time
locating the parking lot for the building.
it wasn't off the main boulevard where
the cars all driven by merciless killers
were doing 55 mph in a 25 mph zone.
the man riding my bumper so
close I could see his snarling face
in my rearview mirror caused me
to miss the narrow alley that would have
allowed me to circle the west
end of the building in search of parking.
I went to the next street, took a right, then
took another right, spotted the building, a blue
heartless-looking structure, then took
another right and finally saw it, a tiny
sign: *parking*.
I drove in.
the guard had the wooden red and white
barrier down.
he stuck his head out a little window.
"yeah?" he asked.
he looked like a retired hit man.
"to see Dr. Manx," I said.
he looked at me disdainfully, then said,
"go ahead!"
the red and white barrier lifted.
I drove in,
drove around and around.
I finally found a parking spot a good distance away,
a football field away.
I walked in.
I finally found the entrance and the elevator
and the floor

and then the office number.
I walked in.
the waiting room was full.
there was an old lady talking to the
receptionist.
"but can't I see him now?"
"Mrs. Miller, you are here at the right time
but on the wrong day.
this is Wednesday, you'll have to come
back Friday."
"but I took a cab. I'm an old lady, I have almost
no money, can't I see him now?"
"Mrs. Miller, I'm sorry but your appointment
is on Friday, you'll have to come back
then."
Mrs. Miller turned away: unwanted,
old and poor, she walked to the
door.
I stepped up smartly, informed them who I was.
I was told to sit down and wait.
I sat with the others.
then I noticed the magazine rack.
I walked over and looked at the magazines.
it was odd: they weren't of recent
vintage: in fact, all of them were over a
year old.
I sat back down.
30 minutes passed.
45 minutes passed.
an hour passed.
the man next to me spoke:
"I've been waiting an hour-and-a-half," he
said.

"that's hell," I said, "they shouldn't do that!"
he didn't reply.
just then the receptionist called my
name.
I got up and told her that the other man had
been waiting an hour-and-a-half.
she acted as if she hadn't heard.
"please follow me," she said.
I followed her down a dark hall, then she
opened a door, pointed. "in there," she said.
I walked in and she closed the door behind me.
I sat down and looked at a map of
the human body hanging from the wall.
I could see the veins, the heart, the
intestines, all that.
it was cold in there and dark, darker
than in the hall.
I waited maybe 15 minutes before the door
opened.
it was Dr. Manx.
he was followed by a tired-looking young lady
in a white gown; she held a clipboard;
she looked depressed.
"well, now," said Dr. Manx, "what is it?"
"it's my leg," I said.
I saw the lady writing on the clipboard.
she wrote LEG.
"what is it about the leg?" asked the Dr.
"it hurts," I said.
PAIN wrote the lady.
then she saw me looking at the clipboard and
turned away.
"did you fill out the form they gave you at

the desk?" the Dr. asked.

"they didn't give me a form," I said.

"Florence," he said, "give him a form."

Florence pulled a form out from her
clipboard, handed it to me.

"fill that out," said Dr. Manx, "we'll be right
back."

then they were gone and I worked at the
form.

it was the usual: name, address, phone,
employer, relatives, etc.

there was also a long list of questions.

I marked them all "no."

then I sat there.

20 minutes passed.

then they were back.

the doctor began twisting my leg.

"it's the *right* leg," I said.

"oh," he said.

Florence wrote something on her
clipboard.

probably RIGHT LEG.

he switched to the right leg.

"does that hurt?"

"a little."

"not real bad?"

"no."

"does *this* hurt?"

"a little."

"not real bad?"

"well, the whole leg hurts but when
you do that, it hurts more."

"but not *real* bad?"

"what's real bad?"
"like you can't stand on it."
"I can stand on it."
"hmmm . . . stand up!"
"all right."
"now, rock on your toes, back and
forth, back and forth."
I did.
"hurt real bad?" he asked.
"just medium."
"you know what?" Dr. Manx asked.
"no."
"we've got a Mystery Leg here!"
Florence wrote something on the
clipboard.
"I have?"
"yes, I don't know yet what's wrong with
it.
I want you to come back in 30 days."
"30 days?"
"yes, and stop at the desk on your
way out, see the girl."
then they walked out.

at the checkout desk there was a long
row of bottles waiting, white bottles with
bright orange labels.
the girl at the desk looked at me.
"take 4 of those bottles."
I did.
she didn't offer me a bag so I stuck
them in my pockets.
"that'll be $143," she said.

"$143?" I asked.
"it's for the pills," she said.
I pulled out my credit card.
"oh, we don't take credit cards," she told
me.
"but I don't have that much money on
me."
"how much do you have?"
I looked in my wallet.
"23 dollars."
"we'll take that and bill you for the
rest."
I handed her the money.
"see you in 30 days," she smiled.
I walked out and into the waiting room.
the man who had been waiting an hour-and-
a-half was still there.
I walked out into the hall, found the
elevator.
then I was on the first floor and out
into the parking lot.
my car was still a football field
away
and my right leg began to hurt like hell,
after all that twisting Dr.
Manx had done to it.
I moved slowly to my car, got in.
it started and soon I was out on the
boulevard again.
the 4 bottles of pills bulged painfully in my
pockets as I drove along.
now I only had one problem left, I had
to tell my wife

I had a Mystery Leg.
I could hear her already:
"what? you mean he couldn't tell
you what was *wrong* with your
leg?
what do you *mean,* he didn't
know?
and what are those PILLS?
here, let me see those!"

as I drove along, I switched on the
radio in search of some soothing
music.

there wasn't any.

be cool, fool

you have to accept this
reality
whether you
sit at a punch press all day or
whether you
work in a coal mine or
whether you come home
exhausted from a cardboard box factory
to find
3 kids bouncing dirty tennis balls
against the walls of a
2 room flat as
your fat wife sleeps while
the dinner burns
away.

you have to accept this
reality
which includes enough nations with
enough nuclear stockpiles to
blow away the very center of the
earth
and to finally liberate
the Devil
Himself
with his
spewing red fire of liquid
doom.

you have to accept this
reality
as the madhouse walls
bulge

break
and the terrified insane
flood our
ugly streets.

you have to accept terrible
reality.

an unliterary afternoon

Roger came by with his well-trimmed beard and puffing his
little pipe.
he taught in the English Dept. at a prestigious university.
Roger was literary in the old-fashioned sense: almost
      every time he opened his mouth you would hear
      "Balzac" or "Hem" or "F. Scott."

I was drinking with Gerda who was also on speed.
Lorraine was passed out in the bedroom but I don't know
what she was on.

Roger sat down with his little smile.
I gave him a can of beer and he drank that and I gave
him another and he began talking away:
"did you know that Céline and Hemingway died on the
same day?"

"no, I didn't know that."

"did you know Whitman might have been a fag?"

"don't believe everything you read."

"hey, who's that babe in your bed?"

"her? that's Lorraine."

after a while Roger got up and
walked into the bedroom and climbed into bed with
Lorraine, shoes and all.
Lorraine didn't seem to notice.

"hey . . . baby!"

Roger reached into her dress and grabbed one of her
breasts.

Lorraine leaped out of bed. *"hey, you son-of-a-bitch! what
do you think you're doing?"*

"oh, I'm sorry . . ."

Lorraine ran into the front room.

"WHO IS THAT SON-OF-A-BITCH? THAT SON-OF-A-BITCH
MOLESTED ME!"

Roger came out of the bedroom. "listen, I'm sorry,
I didn't mean to offend you!"

"YOU KEEP YOUR MOTHERFUCKING HANDS TO YOURSELF, YOU
FUCKING HUNK OF SHIT!"

"yeah," said Gerda, throwing an empty can of beer on the
rug. "go play with yourself!"

Roger walked to the door, opened it, stood there for a moment,
closed it behind him and was
gone.

"WHO WAS THAT PERVERT?" Lorraine asked.

"yeah? who?" asked Gerda.

"that was my friend Roger," I said.

"YEAH? WELL, YOU BETTER TELL HIM TO KEEP HIS HANDS TO
HIMSELF!"

"I will," I told Lorraine.

"I don't know where you get your fucking friends," Gerda said.

"neither do I," I replied.

poop

I remember, he told me, that when I was 6 or
7 years old my mother was always taking me
to the doctor and saying, "he hasn't pooped."

she was always asking me, "have you
pooped?"
it seemed to be her favorite question.
and, of course, I couldn't lie, I had real problems
pooping.
I was all knotted up inside.
my parents did that to me.

I looked at those huge beings, my father,
my mother, and they seemed really stupid.
sometimes I thought they were just pretending
to be stupid because nobody could really be that
stupid.
but they weren't pretending.
they had me all knotted up inside like a pretzel.

I mean, I *had* to live with them, they told
me what to do and how to do it and when.
they fed, housed and clothed me.
and worst of all, there was no other place for
me to go, no other choice:
I had to stay with them.

I mean, I didn't know much at that age
but I could sense that they were lumps
of flesh and little else.

dinnertime was the worst, a nightmare
of slurps, spittle and idiotic conversation.

I looked straight down at my plate and tried
to swallow my food but
it all turned to glue inside.
I couldn't digest my parents or the food.

that must have been it, for it was hell for me
to poop.

"have you pooped?"
and there I'd be in the doctor's office once again.
he had a little more sense than my parents but
not much.

"well, well, my little man, so you haven't pooped?"

he was fat with bad breath and body odor and
had a pocket watch with a large gold chain
that dangled across his gut.

I thought, I bet he poops a load.

and I looked at my mother.
she had large buttocks,
I could picture her on the toilet,
sitting there a little cross-eyed, pooping.
she was so placid, so
like a pigeon.

poopers both, I knew it in my heart.
disgusting people.

"well, little man, you just can't poop,
huh?"

he made a little joke of it: he could,
she could, the world could.
I couldn't.

"well, now, we're going to give you
these pills.
and if they don't work, then guess
what?"

I didn't answer.

"come on, little man, tell me."

all right, I decided to say it.
I wanted to get out of there:

"an enema."

"an enema," he smiled.

then he turned to my mother.
"and are you all right, dear?"

"oh, I'm fine, doctor!"

sure she was.
she pooped whenever she wanted.

then we would leave the office.

"isn't the doctor a nice man?"

no answer from me.

"isn't he?"

"yes."

but in my mind I changed it to, yes,
he can poop.

he looked like a poop.
the whole world pooped while I
was knotted up inside like a pretzel.

then we would walk out on the street
and I would look at the people passing
and all the people had behinds.

"that's all I ever noticed," he told me,
"it was horrible."

"we must have had similar
childhoods," I said.

"somehow, that doesn't help at all,"
he said.

"we've both got to get over this
thing," I said.

"I'm trying," he
answered.

the end of an era

parties at my place were
always marred by
violence:
mine.

it was what
attracted
them: the
would-be
writers
and the
would-be
women.

the writers?
the
women? I could always hear
them
buzzing in the far
corners:

"when's he going to
get mean?
he always
does!"

at all those parties
I enjoyed
the beginnings the
middles

but as each night
unfolded toward
morning

something
somebody
would truly enrage
me

and I'd find myself
picking up some
guy
and
hurling him off the
front porch:

that was
the quickest way to
get rid of
them.

well,
one particular
night
I made up my
mind
to see it
through
to the end
without
untoward
incident

and I was
walking into the
kitchen
for another
drink
when

I was
pounced upon
from
behind
by
Peter the
bookstore
owner.

this bookstore
owner had more
mental problems than
most of
them

and
as he held me
in this excellent
choke-hold from the
rear
his madness gave
him superb
strength

and as the milk-brains
in the other room
babbled on about how to
save the
world

I was being
murdered.

I thought I was
finished.

I saw
bright flashes of
light.

I could no longer
breathe
I felt my heart
beating and my
temples
throb.

like a trapped
animal
I gave it one last
effort

grabbed him
behind the
neck
bent my back
and carried him
like that.

rushed into the
kitchen
ducked my head
low
at the last
moment
and

smashed his skull
against the kitchen
wall.

I steadied myself
a moment
then picked him
up and carried him
into the other
room

and dumped him into
the lap
of his
girlfriend

where from the
safety of her
skirts
this Peter the bookstore
owner
came around and began
crying (yes, he actually
shed tears):

"Hank *hurt* me! he
HURT me! I was only
FOOLING!"

I heard cries of dismay
from around the
room:

"you're a real *bastard*,
Chinaski!"

"Peter sells your books, he
displays them in the
window!"

"Peter LOVES you!"

"O.K.," I said, "everybody
out! FAST!"

sure enough, they filed
out
sharing their
anger and disgust
with one
another.

and
I locked the
door
then
put out the
lights
got myself a
beer
and
sat there
in the dark
drinking
alone.

and
I liked that
so
much
that
that's the way
I continued to

live
from then
on.

there were no more
parties

and
after that
the writing got much
better

everything got much
better
because:

you've got to
get rid of
false friends and
bloodsuckers first
before they
destroy
you.

the 60's

I don't remember much about them
except you'd look and some guy
might be wearing a headdress of Indian
feathers.
everybody was covered with beads
and were passing joints.
they stretched around on comfortable rugs and
didn't do anything.
I don't know how they made the rent.
the woman I was living with was
always telling me, "I'm going to a
Love-In!"
"all right," I'd tell her.
she'd come back and say something
like, "I met this BEAUTIFUL BLACK
MAN!"
or, "we made the cops smile!
I gave one a FLOWER!"
I seemed to be the only person with
an 8-hour job.
and there were always people
coming through the door and raiding
my refrigerator for food and beer.
"WE SHARE!" the woman I lived with
told me, "WE SHARE OUR LOVE!"
a guy would stick his face into mine.
drunk on my beer, he'd scream:
"YOU OUGHTA SEE THE YELLOW
SUBMARINE!"
"what's that?" I asked.
"THE BEATLES, MAN, THE
BEATLES!"
I thought he meant "beetles."

then there was somebody called
WAVY GRAVY.
they even talked me into going on
an LSD trip.
I found it to be stupid.
"you failed," they told me, "you failed,
you didn't open up."
"Peace!" I said, "Peace!"

then, I don't know, all at once
the 60's seemed to be
over.
almost everybody vanished just like
that.

you'd see a few of the leftovers
now and then
down at Venice Beach,
standing around on corners,
sitting on benches
looking really washed-out,
with very vacant stares,
somehow astonished
at the turn of events.
they slept in cars,
stole what they could
and demanded hand-
outs.

I don't know where all the others
went.
I think they got suits and ties

and went looking for
the 8-hour job.
the 70's had arrived.

and that's when *I* dropped out.
and I had the whole place
all to
myself.

the would-be horseplayer

raining, raining, raining.
has been for days.
I have 9 cats, the rain drives them crazy
and then they drive me crazy.
last night at 3:30 one of them began
scratching to get out.
rain and all, he wanted out.
I put him out.
went back to sleep.
then at 4 a.m. the female cat who sleeps in
the bathroom began
mewing.
I sat with her for 5 minutes to calm her down,
then went back to bed.
at 5 a.m. one of the male cats
began scratching.
he had gotten into the closet, found
a bag of cat food, knocked it over and
was trying to claw it open.
I picked him up and put him outside.
I went back to bed and couldn't sleep.
at 8 a.m. I opened a window and a door so
some cats could get back in and some
could get out.
I slept until 10 a.m. when I got up and fed
all 9 cats.

it was time to get ready for the racetrack,
my daily routine.
I stood at the window and watched the rain
still coming down.
it was 20 miles to the track via the freeway and
through a dangerous area—for whites and

maybe blacks too.
I felt sleep deprived so I decided to go back
to bed.
I did, went right to sleep,
and I dreamt.
I dreamt I was at the racetrack.
I was at the betting window, calling my numbers.
it was raining hard.
I was at the racetrack.
I kept betting and I think I cashed some tickets
but I never saw a horse or a jockey or a horse race.
then I awakened.

it was still raining.
my wife (who is an insomniac) was
sleeping peacefully next to me and there were
4 cats sleeping on the bed and
one on the floor.
we were all sleep deprived.
I looked at the clock: 12:30, too late to make
the track.

I turned on my right side, looked out the
window.
it was still raining, heartlessly,
hopefully, meanly, grossly, continually,
beautifully.
rain, rain, rain, rain, rain, rain.
soon I was asleep again and the world continued to do
very well without
me.

the night Richard Nixon shook my hand

I was up there on the platform,
ready to begin when
up walked Richard Nixon
(or his double)
with that familiar
glazed smile on his face.
he approached me, reached out and
before I could react he
shook my hand.
what is he doing? I thought.
I was about to give him a verbal
dressing down
but before I could do so
he suddenly faded away
and all I could see were the
lights shining in my eyes and
the audience waiting down
there.

my hand was shaking as
I reached out and poured myself
a glass of vodka from the pitcher.

I must be giving this poetry reading
in hell, I thought.

it *was* hell: I drained the glass
but the contents somehow had turned into
water.

I began to read the first poem:
"I wandered lonely as a cloud."

Wordsworth!

throwing away the alarm clock

my father always said, "early to bed and
early to rise makes a man healthy, wealthy
and wise."

it was lights out at 8 p.m. in our house
and we were up at dawn to the smell of
coffee, frying bacon and scrambled
eggs.

my father followed this general routine
for a lifetime and died young, broke,
and, I think, not too
wise.

taking note, I rejected his advice and it
became, for me, late to bed and late
to rise.

now, I'm not saying that I've conquered
the world but I've avoided
numberless early traffic jams, bypassed some
common pitfalls
and have met some strange, wonderful
people

one of whom
was
myself—someone my father
never
knew.

pretenders

nothing is worse than
a hopelessly untalented
entertainer.

unlike the talented
they have boundless
exuberance and no
self-doubt.

luckily, for us,
we seldom encounter
one of them
except
sometimes
at small parties
or as entertainers
in
cheap cafes.

you don't have to actually
go to hell
to know what hell must be
like: just looking
at
and listening to
one of them
gives you a
good
idea.

there seems to be
one simple undying
rule:

the worse the
talent
the more they
are sure
of
it.

$1.25 a gallon

life can be vacant like the inside of
old shoes while dogs howl in the
rain.
sometimes a certain anger is necessary to
stay alive.
I drive into the gas station
in my '67 Volks and
there's a woman parked ahead of
me.
I honk
she looks back.
I honk again
make a motion with my hand
for her to get out and pour some
gas into her tin buggy. she looks
astonished.
it's a cut-rate self-serve gas station
and
we all suffer the long lines of
merciless doom.
the attendant finally comes out and
handles her
affairs. she tells him about me:
I am a bastard—no style, no
decency.
I
look at her ass
decide I don't like it
much. she looks at my face and
decides the same. as she
drives off I lift the
hood
grab the nozzle and think,

maybe she was out to fuck me;
I just didn't feel in the mood
for it.
when the attendant walks up
I see by his face
that he felt the same way.
I pay, ask him directions
to Beverly Hills and drive off
into the sick drooping
pink sun.

floss-job

that dental assistant in
Burbank
a few years
back
so dedicated

cleaning my teeth

leaning against
me
her large breasts
pressed against my arm and
shoulder

her eyes
looking into
mine
asking

"does this
hurt?"

I still think about
her golden breasts.

she probably told
her girlfriends about it
later,
laughing her ass
off:
"I turned-on this old
fuck.
Christ, it was like

raising the
dead.
his old dried dick
waving in the
air.
his rotting mouth
hoping for
one last kiss!"

yes, dear, it hurts
but our dumb peasant wedding
was greater than
you know.

a friendly place

went into this sushi place to eat.
sat at the counter.
2 fellows to my left.
one of them asked me, "what's
that beer you're drinking?"
I told him.
he said that his beer was better,
that he'd buy me one.
"no thanks," I said.
"how about a sake?"
"thank you very much, but no."
"have you ever tried
octopus?"
"no."
"here, try some of mine."
"yeah, try some!" said his friend.
"thanks, but no."
"no, here! here! try it!"
he put a piece on my plate.
I picked it up and began to chew.
it tasted like a piece of rubber.
"you like it?"
"it tastes like rubber."
there was a pause, then
"we live on a boat," said the nearest
speaker.
"in the harbor," said the other.
"try some sake," said the first.
"no, thanks."
"you live on a boat?" the other
asked.
"no."
"we bought you a beer anyway," they said,

"here it is, try it."
"ah, thank you."
I took a hit.
"good, yes, thank you."
"want some more octopus?"
"no thanks, you're very kind."
"we live on a boat," the first said.
I continued eating.
"you live around here?" he
asked.
"yes."
"where?"
"in town."
"where in town?"
"near first and Bandini."
"you know Peaches? she lives
on Bandini."
"I know her, she gives loud parties."
"she's married to my brother."
"oh, good."
"Peaches is a great girl!"
"yeah."
"I'm going to buy you a sake."
"no, thanks."
"how come?"
"I drink too much, I start to roll."
"rock and roll?"
"no, just roll."
"everybody comes to the parties on our
boat, but when
the food and booze are
gone, they leave."
"they do?"

"yeah, then we gotta do all the clean
up ourselves!"
a long pause.
I continued eating, then said,
"well, listen, thanks for the beer,
I've got to go."
"where you going?"
"home."
"we're having a party on the boat
tonight . . ."
"good."
"what'd you say your name
was?"
"Hank," I said.
"I'm Bob."
"I'm Eddie."
I walked around the counter to
pay.
then as I walked back to exit:
"don't you want one for the
road?" Bob asked.
"no, thanks a lot, though."
"see you around," said Eddie.
"sure," I said.

then I was outside.
I walked back to my car
thinking, well, anyhow,
now I can tell people that I
have eaten
octopus.

the old couple

about ten minutes before the last race they were walking
through the parking lot to their car, he walking in front
by a good four feet, his head turned back toward her
as he walked and talked.
"why did we have to sit in that crowded section?
I never want to sit there again! I couldn't
concentrate!"
and she replied, "oh, shut up, Harry."

he kept walking, talking with his head turned: "I TOLD you in advance
I wouldn't be able to CONCENTRATE there!"

and she said,
"oh, go on, go on, you always make some
EXCUSE!"

he stopped.
she stopped. they stared at each
other.

"god damn it," he said, "YOU take the car! I'm going to take
a taxi!"

and she said,
"now, don't do anything FOOLISH, don't be
STUPID!"

then they started walking again with the same four feet
of space between them.

in the distance
the call to post sounded for the last
race.

"who'd you bet in the
9th?" she asked.

he replied, "that's MY own
god-damned
business!"

then I started the engine of my
car and could hear
no more.

what?

I was already old and hadn't made it
as a writer
when a young man sitting on my couch
asked me,
"what do you think of Huxley living up
in the Hollywood hills while you live down
here?"
"I don't think anything about it,"
I told him.
"what do you mean?" he asked.
"I mean, I don't think it has anything
to do with anything."

now the young man who asked me
that question lives up in the hills
and I still live down here
and I still don't think it has anything
to do with
anything.
especially with writing.
but people keep asking foolish
questions,
don't
they?

born again

this special place of ourselves
sometimes explodes in our
faces.
I got a flat on the freeway yesterday,
changed the right rear wheel on the
shoulder,
the big rigs storming by,
slamming the sky
against my head and
body.
it felt like I was clinging to the
edge of the earth,
30 minutes late for the first
post.

but strangely, something
about the experience
was very much like emerging reluctantly
a second time
from my
mother's womb.

card girls

at the prizefights
between each round a card girl
climbs up into the ring
holding up a card to
indicate the number of the next
round.
the yowling of the men is
hardly to be
believed.

here were brave fighters
putting their lives and guts
on the line
and the crowd responds much more
enthusiastically
to female
ass.

why not give the crowd just one
card girl after another and
forget all about the fighters?

then those men could simply sit and
fantasize about having one
of those card girls
all to himself
in his bedroom.
he then would not have
to deal with such things
as PMS, relatives, self-
love, ambition, the fact that she
was only a bundle of intestine and
other sundry parts, or remember that

card girls must be faithfully and
continually adored
for the beauty they had never
earned.

yes, give them each a card girl
forever shaking her butt,
each man with a card girl
in his bedroom forever
fucking her forever
bang bang bang
nothing but that—
no fights, no farts, no
dark nights, no cousins, no mothers,
no other lovers, no pregnancies, no
madness while gradually growing
old, no toothaches, no snoring,
no dull endless tv nights,
just one perfect card girl for each
man,
bang, bang, bang,
sperm and endless desire and the dream
forever, one card girl for each
horny man, forget the fighters,
forget everything
else!
yeah.

I left while the last fight
was still in progress,
the 6 card girls
sitting in their fold-
ing chairs, their faces

somehow looking
more beautiful than ever
but
mirroring a horror to
come.

outside as I moved to
my car
the night was clear and crisp and
real.

well, I thought, maybe you're
just too old to understand.

I smiled at that as I slid
my key into
the car
door.

it's never been so good

it isn't mentioned
too often
but in the old West
many men were simply shot in
the back.

this matter of bravely facing
each other
in the street
and drawing their guns
was
rare.

the best shooter was
usually
the one who
pulled his gun and
fired first
while the other was
having a drink
or eating
or playing cards
or bedded down with
a lady
or
otherwise
occupied.

"dead men don't talk,"
they used to
say.

in the new West
things haven't changed
at all

just the weaponry:
now they can get in 17 or 18
or
more
shots in the back
quicker than you can say
holy
shit.

goading the muse

this man used to be an
interesting writer,
he was able to say brisk and
refreshing things.
at the time
I suggested to the editors and
the critics that he was one to
be watched
and also that he had hardly yet been
noticed
and that he certainly should now be
noticed.
this writer used some of my
remarks as blurbs for his
books, which I didn't
mind.
all of his publications were little
chapbooks, 16 to 32
pages,
mimeographed.
they came out at a
rapid rate,
perhaps three or four a
year.
the problem was that each
chapbook seemed a little weaker
than the one that preceded
it
but he continued to use my old
blurbs.
my wife noticed the change
in his writing
too.

"what's happened to his
writing?" she asked me.
"he's doing too much of it, he's
pushing it out, forcing it."
"this stuff is bad, you ought to
tell him to stop using your
blurbs."
"I can't do that, I just wish he
wouldn't publish so much."
"well, you publish all the
time too."
"with me," I told her, "it's
different."

yesterday I received another of his
little chapbooks
with his delicate dedication scrawled
on the title page.
this latest effort was totally
flat.
the words just fell off the
page,
dead on
arrival.

where had he gone?

too much ambition?
too much just doing it for the sake
of doing it?
just not waiting for the words to
pile up inside and then
explode of their own
volition?

I decided then I should take a whole week
off,
be on the safe side,
just shut the computer down,
forget the whole damned silly
business
for awhile.

as I said, that was
yesterday.

the wavering line

I don't know where they come from,
the veterans' home probably.
they're old, mostly bald, tanned, macho but
somehow sexless.
the sex drive is no longer a part
of the equation as
they sit at the track in the sun,
arguing about their bets, talking and
laughing.
sometimes between races they
discuss sports: which is the best?
the best baseball team? the best
hockey team? the best basketball or
football team? amateurs and
professionals are discussed, and then
who's the best player at each
position?
they often become angry and shout
at one another.

they wear tired clothing, greys and
browns, they wear heavy shoes and
each sports a large wristwatch,
and while other men only
slightly younger than themselves still must
fight for survival
in the arena of daily existence
they sit about and argue
whether the screen pass is still
an effective offensive weapon in professional
football.

they bet, first gathering in front of the
window, arguing, making last minute

adjustments, then one of them bets for
all of them.
after the races end each
evening they leave,
a wavering line,
some stumbling a bit as if
they were tripping over their own
feet.
now they look worn and done,
defeated.

"shit, this god-damned place, catch
me here again and you can belt-whip me
until I sing Dixie!"

"yeah, sure, Marty, you'll be back tomorrow."

"naw. fuck this place!"

the next afternoon they are all back,
somehow they've found a small supply of
new money—they will pool it and their brains
and do it all over again today.
they are suddenly serious, studying their
Racing Forms.

they bet the first two races and things go
wrong. the conversation jumps angrily from
horses to sports and the screaming
begins:
"YEAH, YOU KNOW WHAT? I'LL BET YOU
NEVER HEARD OF CRAZYLEGS
HIRSCH!"
"I SAW HIM, MAN! I SAW HIM PLAY!"

"YEAH? WELL, I SAW JIM THORPE!"
"YEAH? YOU SAW JIM THORPE JUST LIKE YOU
GOT LAID LAST NIGHT!"
"YEAH, I NOTICE *YOU* CAN HARDLY SIT DOWN TODAY!
DID YOU GET LAID LAST NIGHT?"
"I'LL KNOCK YOUR GOD-DAMNED HEAD OFF!"

the combat never evolves and that's all well
and good, for they are fine fellow, we
need them like we need the Sierra Madre mountains
choking behind us in the smog, like we need
Willie Shoemaker legging it up on just
one more winner, and we need them to help us
forget all the things that haven't worked out for us
in the past, especially all the bad bets.
what counts is to endure, what counts
is not to remember that the whole western slope
of the U.S.A. is going to fall into the Pacific Ocean
one day soon
and that there was never any real need to cultivate your
garden or to send your daughter to
Radcliffe.

I like to watch those fellows, they are
like a Broadway musical, only it's not
Guys and Dolls it's *Guys and Guys,* they
are all fine fellows, the wavering line of
them, and even the most beautiful woman in the
world would mean nothing to them
because they have learned the hard way
that that kind of thing only
exists for other people, and there's
just no use wondering how things got that way or
why.

I watch the best Broadway musical
every day from the best seat in the
house and I am the author and the critic and the
audience and sometimes I'm on stage
too.

the road to hell

if only there were more magic people
to help us get through
this strange life.

surprisingly there are a few.

the problem being that often
their magic doesn't hold up
for long
mainly
because they begin to
think it's because
they are special

when really
it's almost an off-hand thing
like some damned crazy unearned
gift.

and when the magic people
begin to misuse their
prowess
begin to use it
in the wrong ways
then
it
vanishes

and
that's a
LAW

and
it's one of the most

unalterable laws
of the gods and the
universe

and there is
nothing sadder
or more
frightening
than the once-gifted ones
still trying to work their
magic
for the
crowd

which never offers,
but only
accepts,
mercy.

crucifixion

now we must select with extreme caution our lovers,
water, foodstuffs and even our invisible
air.

it is a very careful time.

our politicians consider ways to dismantle
the worldwide stockpile of bombs
all too late, of course, since it only takes one fool to
push one button
somewhere.

we draw close together, frightened, searching for a return
to a safe
womb.

but we must have been wrong for too long. the asylums overflow and
        spill their
detritus into our streets
and where our leaders once spoke wisely
they now speak gibberish—
they stop, then continue, look about, addled,
substituting insane slogans for real
speech.

this is the price we now pay: we can't go
back, we can't go forward and we hang helpless, nailed to a
world
of our own
making.

barfly

Jane, who has been dead for 31 years,
never could have
imagined that I would write a screenplay of our drinking
days together
and
that it would be made into a movie
and
that a beautiful movie star would play her
part.

I can hear Jane now: "A beautiful movie star? oh,
for Christ's sake!"

Jane, that's show biz, so go back to sleep, dear, because
no matter how hard they tried they
just *couldn't* find anybody exactly like
you.

and neither can
I.

bone–dead sorrows
like starfish washed ashore.

thoughts while eating a sandwich

we demand that our leaders possess
a certain clever charm, a certain mild wisdom, but no madness,
at least not madness at its
best.
maybe the energy is just not there anymore, maybe
not only is the air polluted, maybe the brain has been
poisoned, maybe the human spirit has been
diluted down to a dim imitation of
itself
until anybody who appears half-right half-the-time is
almost always accepted as our new
hero-leader.

it is more and more difficult—no, it's just damned
impossible—to accept and admire those who are
deemed great in our time.
they all
are suspect
they all seem to lack:
nobility
originality
intelligence
honesty
and especially that which is most needed:
a simple, good heart.

just bones and more bones
bleaching in the sun.

they say that nothing is wasted:
either that
or
it all is.

nothing's free

got this letter
where she wrote:
I'm not going to do the obvious and
throw in a photo
but don't worry
I've got a BODY
and the face
is not so bad
either.
anyhow, I really admire
your books although
I just discovered them
recently.
you see I am
only 18 years old but
I'd like to be your
secretary
kind of keep house for you
answer the phone
all that
and just room and board
would do—
no salary
and
I wouldn't ask you
for sex
unless you asked me
first . . .

you can be sure
I tossed that letter
into the
trash can
right away.

what bothers them most

Sandra used to phone me almost
nightly.

"what are you doing?"

"nothing."

"you mean, you aren't *with*
anybody yet?"

"no."

"why not?"

"who needs it?"

(I hang up)

they simply never understand,
do they,
that sometimes solitude is
one of the most beautiful things
on earth?

(then the phone rings again,
a few nights later)

"well, are you *with* anybody yet?"

"no."

"why don't you ask me if I'm
with somebody?"

"are you with somebody?"

"not now, but I've been going out
with Tim."

"Tim's a good guy, tell him
I said 'hello'."

(I hang up)

I found my nights to be perfectly
pleasant and the day as pleasant
too.
I typed and laughed my ass
off
then strapped it back on and
typed some
more.

one night
while I was
typing and
laughing my ass off
I heard high heels
coming
up the walk.

then there was only silence
so I took a hit of my
drink and typed
some more.

suddenly there was a
crash and
the breaking of

glass
and
a large rock
rolled
across the rug
and stopped
just next to
where I was
sitting.

I heard high heels
running back
down the walk,
then
the sound
of a car
starting,
then
driving off with
a
roar.

a pane of glass was
missing
from the
front door.

Sandra phoned
two nights later.

"how are you doing?"

"fine."

"why don't you ask me
how *I'm*
doing?"

"o.k., all right, how
are you
doing?"

"YOU ROTTEN SON OF
A BITCH!" she
screamed and
hung up.

however
this time
there was somebody
there with me.

"who was that?"
she asked.

"a voice from the
past."

"oh, well,
may we continue with
our
interview?
what is the principal
inspiration for your
poetry?"

"fucking."

"*what?*"

"FUCKING," I repeated
loudly,
then walked over
and
refilled her shaking
drink.

into the wastebasket

my father liked to pretend he
would some day be wealthy.
he always voted Republican
and he told me that
if I worked hard
every day of my life that
I would be amply
rewarded.

on those occasions
when my father *had* a
job he worked hard, he
worked so hard that nobody
could stand him.

"what's the matter with that
man? is he crazy?"

my father was a sweating
red-faced
angry
man
and it seemed that the
harder he tried
the poorer he
became.
his blood pressure
rose
and his heartbeat was
irregular.
he smoked Camels and
Pall Malls and
half-full packs were scattered

everywhere.
he was asleep by
8 p.m. and up at
5 a.m. and
he tended to scream at and
beat his wife and
child.

he died early.
and after his funeral
I sat in the bedroom of his empty
house
smoking his last pack of
Pall Malls.

he believed that there was
only one formula, one way:
his.

it wasn't shameful for him to
die, it was his unbending attitude
toward life
that bothered me
and I spoke to him
about it once
and told him
that life was just
rather sad and
empty
and all we could hope
for
was to enjoy a few moments
of peace and quiet

amidst the
turmoil.

"you just sit on your
ass," he replied, "you and
your mouth!"
well, *I* say the answer is
'a good day's
work for a good day's
pay!' "

come to think of it,
if I was unhappy
it wasn't completely
my father's fault
and after I smoked the last
Pall Mall cigarette
in that last pack
I threw it away
and then
he too was finally
gone
for
good.

it's over and done

sensibly adorned with its iron cross
the red fokker sails my brain
and
as my father opens a door from hell
    and screams my name
up from below
I know that it is time to
accept what is true:
while there can be no
    reconciliation
between us
to carp about old wounds is
    a stupid waste of the heart.

sensibly adorned with its iron cross
the red fokker flies away
and disappears over Brazil
and I close my eyes
as
the light fails in the eye of the
    falcon,
and the useless anger of the living
for the dead
is
    lost
    forever.

nice guy

I broke his bank, totaled his car and slept with
his wife.
of course, everybody was sleeping with his
wife but a nicer guy you never
met.
T.K. Kemper played a couple of years with
the Green Bay Packers
then a bad knee got him.
he went into automotive repair,
did very good work.
he was a
lousy card player though; we'd get him
drunk and take it all from
him,
his wife lurking in the background, her tits
hanging out.
T.K. Kemper.
big, big guy.
hands like hams.
honest blue eyes.
give you the shirt off his back.
give you his back if he could.
one night after work he saw two punks
snatch a purse from an old
lady.
he ran after them trying to get that purse
back.
he was gaining on them when
one of the punks turned, had a gun, fired
5 shots.
he was a big, big guy.
he caught all 5 shots, hit the pavement
hard, didn't move.

there was a good crowd at the funeral.
his wife cried.
my friend Eddie consoled her,
then took her home and fucked
her.

T.K. Kemper.
bad knee.
good heart.

he was not meant for this indifferent world.

only with supreme luck did he last
29 years.

feet to the fire

June, late night, common pain like a rat trapped in
the gut, how brave we are to continue walking through this terrible
flame
as
the sun stuns us
as a dark flood envelops us as
we go on our way—
filling the gas tank, flushing toilets, paying bills—as we
float in our pain
kick our feet
wiggle our toes
while listening to inept melodies
that float in the air
as the agony now eats the soul.
yes, I think we're admirable and brave but we should have
quit
long ago, don'tcha
think?

yet
here we sit
uncorking a new
bottle and listening to
Shostakovitch.
we've died so many times now that we can only wonder why we still
care.

so
I pour this drink for
all of us

and
pour another
for
myself.

the poetry game

the boys
are playing the poetry game
again
putting down
meaningless lines
and
passing them off as art
again.

the boys
are on the telephone
again
writing letters
again
to the publishers and
editors
telling them
who to edit and who to
publish.

the boys
know that either you
belong or you
don't.

there's a way to do it
you see
and
only a few know how to
do it
the right way.

all the others
are *out*

and
if you don't know
who's out
or
who's in
well
the boys
will tell you
again.

the boys
have been around a
long time:
for a couple of
centuries
at least.

and before some of
the old boys
die
they pass their wisdom on
to the younger
boys
so *they* can put down
meaningless lines
and
pass them off as art
again.

the fix is in

children in the school yard, the horrors they must
endure as they are first shaped for life to come and then
handed a hopeless future consisting of:
false hope
cheap patriotism
minimum-wage jobs
(or no
job at all)
mortgages and car payments
an indifferent government—
the days, nights, years all finally pointing to the
dissolution of any possible
chance.

as I wait in the car wash for my automobile
I watch the children in the school yard to the west
playing at recess.

then a little old man waves a
rag and whistles.
my car is
ready.

I walk to my car, tip the old
fellow: "how's it
going?"

"o.k.," he answers, "I'm hoping for it to
rain."

just then the school bell rings and the children stop
playing and troop into the large brick
building.

"I hope it rains too,"
I say as I climb in and drive
away.

photos

I have a photo of Baron Manfred Von Richthofen
standing with his buddies
and there's his fighter plane in the background
and further down on the wall
there's a photo of a red
three-winged fokker in
flight.

the few people who come into this
room (where I
work at night)
have seen these things
but don't say
anything.

that's o.k.
but between you and me
things like that
got me through a childhood
that was less than
pleasant.

after that, it was then up to
me.
but I still don't mind having old
friends
like this
still hanging around.

tonight

so many of my brain cells eaten away by
alcohol
I sit here drinking now
all of my drinking partners dead,
I scratch my belly and dream of the
albatross.
I drink alone now.
I drink with myself and to myself.
I drink to my life and to my death.
my thirst is still not satisfied.
I light another cigarette, turn the
bottle slowly, admire
it.
a fine companion.
years like this.
what else could I have done
and done so well?
I have drunk more than the first
one hundred men you will pass
on the street
or see in the madhouse.
I scratch my belly and dream of the
albatross.
I have joined the great drunks of
the centuries.
I have been selected.
I stop now, lift the bottle, swallow a
mighty mouthful.
impossible for me to think that
some have actually stopped and
become sober
citizens.
it saddens me.

they are dry, dull, safe.
I scratch my belly and dream of the
albatross.
this room is full of me and I am
full.
I drink this one to all of you
and to me.
it is past midnight now and a lone
dog howls in the
night.
and I am as young as the fire that still
burns
now.

a visitor complains

"hey, man," he said, "I liked your poems better when you were
puking and living with whores and hitting the bars and ending
up in the drunk tank and getting into alley
fights."

then
he went on to talk about and read his own down-to-earth
poems.

II

what some poets and pundits don't realize is how ridiculous it is
to cling forever to the same subject
matter.

in time the whores wear thin: their hard
vision, their curses, their tiny endearments become more than
deadly.

and as for puking you can soon get too much of
that
especially when it leads to a stinking bed in the
charity ward.

and as for alley fights I was never too good a
warrior, I was only seeing if I had a touch of courage—
I found some, and finding that, there was no further need to
explore.

I mean, you can describe a harsh lifestyle in your poems but sooner
or later you will find it's time to move on. if you hang on
too long the subject matter gets thin and tiresome and, yes,
I still love my booze but

I can pass on the whores, the bars and the drunk tanks without
        feeling that
I have sold my god-damned soul down the bloody dung-filled
river.

some pundits would be delighted if my poems again found me
in some skid row alley with
face bashed in and the flies swarming the emptiness of me.

some pundits
need Van Gogh madness and Mozart suffering to feed on
or
Dostoevsky with his back to the firing wall.
some pundits consider misfortune to be the
only viable art–
form.

as for Van Gogh, Mozart, Dostoevsky, etc.
I say that they did neither choose nor welcome their
pain and suffering.

III
of course, I didn't tell this to my poet-visitor
he was too busy
belching and farting and woofing and poofing
gurgling the libations I offered him
as he read me his *own* exploits in the almighty
gutter
which were hardly believable
and bordered on farce.

that loud voice
those hairy eyebrows

that delight in personal misfortune—
as if living badly was a triumph and
a very proud
accomplishment.

his feet planted flat upon my floor
he gave me the gut-pain he claimed was so very
necessary and
grand.

besieged

you see, this wall is green and that wall is
blue and the 3rd wall has eyes and
the last wall is crawling with angry famished
spiders.

no, that wall is a sheet of frozen water
and the other is one of melting wax
and the 3rd frames my grandmother's face
and from the 4th spills the bones of my father.

outside is the city, the city outside, a thing that
creeps to the call of bells and lights,
the city is an open grave,
so I never dare to venture forth but
rather remain and hide within
disconnect the phone
lower the shades and
cut the
lights.

the city is more cruel than the walls
and finally the walls are all we have
and
almost nothing is
far better than
nothing at
all.

the novice

early one morning, during the Depression,
in the railroad yard, when I was 20 years old,
I walked alone along the Union Pacific tracks.
I was apprehensive as
on the first day on that job
I walked to where we all checked in.
3 dark figures stood in the way
expressionless faces
legs spread a bit;
as I got closer one of them grabbed his crotch
the other 2 leered;
I walked quickly up to them and
at the last moment they parted.
I walked past them
stopped and
turned: "I'll take on any one of you
one at a time.
anybody
want to try it now?"

nobody moved
nobody spoke
I walked over
found my timecard in the rack and
punched in.

the foreman came over
his face even uglier than mine.
he said: "listen, we do our work around here
we don't want any trouble-makers."

I went to work.

later while I was scrubbing down a boxcar
with water and an oakite brush

the leader of that gang came up and
said: "listen, man, we're going to get you."
"maybe," I said, "but it won't be easy."

it wasn't bad work
the hangover had worn off
and I liked the way the oakite brush dissolved the grime;
also the cheap bars of the coming night beckoned to me
and there was always a bottle of wine waiting in my room.

at noon in the mess hall
when I got up to put a coin in the soft drink machine
all 3 stopped talking and watched.

but as days and weeks went on
nothing ever happened.

I gave that job six weeks then took a Trailways bus to New Orleans
and looking out the window at all that empty, wasted land
while sucking at a pint of
Cutty Sark
I wondered when and where
I might finally come to rest and then
fit in.

Cleopatra now

she was one of the most beautiful actresses
of our time
once married to a series of
rich and famous men
and now she is in traction, in hospital, a fractured
back, the painkillers at work.
she is now 60
and only a few years ago
her room would have been bursting with flowers,
the phone ringing, many visitors on the waiting
list.

now, the phone seldom rings, there
are only a few obligatory flowers,
and visitors are at a
minimum.

yet, with age the lady has matured, she knows more now, understands
more, feels more deeply, relates to life much more
kindly.

all to no avail: if you are no longer a good young
fuck, if you can't play the
temptress with
legs crossed high and
violet eyes glowing
behind
long dark lashes,
if you're not still beautiful
if you ain't in movies any longer
if you aren't photographed drunk and obnoxious
in the best
restaurants with new young

lovers:
it's all to no
avail.

now she sits forgotten
in hospital
straddling a bedpan
as new horizons open up for
the new generation.

in traction you're pathetic at 60
and
nobody wants to sit in a room with
you.
it's too
depressing.

this world wants only the young and the strong and the
still beautiful.

as this once-famous actress
lies forgotten in hospital
I wonder what thoughts she
has
about her x-lovers
about her x-public
about her vanished youth
as the hours and the days
crawl
by.

I truly wonder what thoughts she
has.

possibly she has discovered her real self,
achieved real wisdom.
but has it come too late?
and when late wisdom
finally arrives
is that better than none at
all?

please

in the night now thinking of the years and the
women gone and lost forever
not minding the women gone, not even minding the years
lost forever
if
we could just have some peace now—a year of peace, a month of
peace, a week of peace—
not peace for the world—just a selfish bit of peace
for me
to loll in like in green warm
water, just a bit of it, just an hour of it, some
peace, yes, in the night in the night while thinking of
the years lost and the women gone in this night in this very long
dark and lonely
night.

the barometer

your critics are always going to be
there
and the more successful you become
the more criticism you'll
receive
especially from those
who are most desperate
for a taste of the same success
you have
achieved.

but the thing you must always remember
regardless of the criticism
is to try to continue to get
better at whatever it is that
you do.

I think what bothers the critics the most
however
is to see someone succeed
after coming out of
nowhere
instead of from their very
special circle of the waiting-to-be-
annointed.

critics and failed creators
dominate the landscape
and the more you successfully harness
the natural power of your
art
the more they are going to
insist

through intrigue and
through their rankling
pitiful
malice

that
you were never very much
to begin with
and that now, of course, you're even
less than
that.

the critics are always going to be
there and
when they stop, if ever, then
you will know
that your own brief day in the sun
is over.

enemy of the king, 1935

I kept looking at him and thinking,
the ears don't fit and the mouth
is foolish and the eyes are wrong.
his shoes don't look right and his tone of
voice is an insult.
his shirt hangs from his shoulders
as if it dislikes him.
he chews his food like a dog
and look at that Adam's apple!
and why are his favorite subjects
"money" and "work"?
why does he splash angrily
in the bathtub
when he bathes?
and why does he hate me?
and why do I hate him?
why are we enemies?
why does he look like a fool?
how can I get away from him?

"WHAT THE HELL ARE YOU LOOKING
AT?" he screams.
"GO TO YOUR ROOM!
I'LL DEAL WITH YOU LATER!"

"have it your way."
"WHAT?"
"have it your way."

"YOU CAN'T TALK TO ME LIKE
THAT!
GO TO YOUR ROOM!"

the room was beautiful.
I couldn't see him anymore.

I couldn't hear his voice.
I looked at the dresser.
the dresser was beautiful.
I looked at the rug.
the rug was beautiful.
I sat in a chair and waited.

hours passed.

it was dark.
now he was listening to the
radio
in the living room.

I kicked the screen open and
dropped out the window.
then I was out in the cool night,
walking.

I was 15 years old,
looking for something,
anything.

it wasn't there.

nights of vanilla mice

unshaven, yellow-toothed, sweating in my only shorts
and undershirt (full of cigarette holes),
I was sure that I was better than F. Scott or Faulkner or
even my buddy, Turgenev.
ah, not as good as Céline or Li Po
but, man, I had faith, felt I was more on fire
than
any 3 dozen mortals.
and I typed and lived with women that you
would shrink from, I
brought love back to those faded eyes as vanilla mice
slept below our bed.
I starved and starved and typed and
loved it, I
reached into my mouth and plucked rotten teeth
out of my gums
and laughed
as the rejections came back as fast as I could send my stories
out, I
felt marvelous, I felt like I owned a piece of the
sun, I listened to all the crazy classical music from previous
centuries, I sympathized with those who had suffered
in the past like
Mozart, Verdi, others,
and when things got really bad
I thought of Van Gogh and his ear and even
sometimes
his shotgun, I
jollied myself along as best I could, and Jesus I
got very *thin*
and still during the sleepless nights I would
tell my ladies about how I was
going to make it as a writer some day

and from all of them (as if with one voice) they would complain:
"shit, are you going to talk about *that*
again?"
(my voice): "you saw how I punched that guy out
in the alley the other night?"
(again, as with one voice): "what has that to do with
writing?"
(my voice): "I don't know . . ."

of course, there were many nights with no voices,
there were many nights alone and those were fine
too, of course, but the worst nights were the nights
without a room and that hurt because a writer needed
an address in order to receive those rejection
slips.

but the ladies (bless them!)
always told me, "you're crazy but you're
nice."

being a starving writer is
treacherous
great
fun.

lark in the dark

all teeth, big nose
coming directly at me
in the middle of the night.
I am frozen in the bed
as it comes roaring down at me
from the ceiling.
I roll away at the last
moment
and it hits the bed
between me and my white
cat.
the cat jumps straight up,
hits the ceiling,
bounces back, hits the
bed, leaps off, jumps through
the screen and lands two floors
below in the Jacuzzi.
I get up, watch it swim to the
edge, crawl out.
it sits there licking itself in the
moonlight.
"whatcha doin'?" I hear my wife
say.
"gotta go to the bathroom,"
I tell her.
I walk to the bathroom,
come back,
climb under the
covers.
"don't snore," says my wife.
I stare at the spot in the ceiling
from where the apparition first
appeared.

for two hours I do this.
then I am asleep again.
I am dreaming.
I am naked and driving one of
those old-fashioned steam locomotives
through a shopping
mall.
I smile and wave
to the crowds but
nobody seems to notice
me.

lonely hearts

when you start boring yourself
you know damn well
you're going to start
boring other people;
in fact, all the people you come
into contact with:
on the telephone, in the post
office, over a bowl of
spaghetti.

oh, all the tiresome people with their
tiresome stories:
like how they got screwed by life's
Unkind Forces, how they are fucked
and there isn't much they can do
now
except tell you all about it.

then they step back and wait for
you to console them
but what you really feel like doing
is
piss all over them,
which might stop them from
inviting themselves over for
dinner
and then telling you more about
their tragic
lives.

there are more and more of
them,
they line up outside in the gloom

waiting for you.
nobody else will listen to
them.
they've alienated
hundreds of former
friends, lovers and acquaintances
but they still need to whine and
complain.

I'm sending them all over to
see you
starting today.
get your compassion and
understanding
ready.

I might be there at the end of that
line
myself.

B as in bullshit

B kind
B a good listener
B able to engage in physical combat
B a lover of classical music
B a tolerator of children
B a good horseplayer
B an agnostic
B generous on the freeways of the world
B a good sleeper
B not fearful of death
B unable to beg
B able to love
B able to feel superior
B able to understand that too much education is a fart in the dark
B able to dislike poets and poetry
B able to understand that the rich can be poor in spirit
B able to understand that the poor live better than the rich
B able to understand that shit is necessary
B aware that in every life a little bit of shit must fall
B aware that a hell of a lot more shit falls on some more than on
        others
B aware that many dumb bastards crawl the earth
B aware that the human heart cannot be broken
B able to stay away from movies
B able to sit alone in a room and feel good
B able to watch your cat cross the floor like a miracle
B able to recognize bullshit even when you hear it from
B ukowski.

a riot in the streets

it's a good day, a good time, anybody can
blow a hole through you at any minute.

they are shooting from the rooftops now
and the night sky is smoking,
red.

what more could you want?
you can watch it on your tv or you
can look outside, it's the same
thing.

they are letting it all out again.
airing it out.
it's healthy.

the cops are hiding.
nobody is bored tonight.
the safest people are already in jail.

everybody feels curiously alive,
at last.

it's party time!

this city is the whole world
and it's running right at you.

it's a good day, a good time!

hell is coming out to play

with you.

interlude

it's been raining forever
and I haven't had a drink in
a week-and-a-half.
I must be going crazy.
I just sit in these green pajamas
smoke cigars and stare at the walls.
I try to read the newspapers but
the print blurs and I can't
make sense out of any of
it.
I watch the second hand
go around and around on my
watch.
I am waiting for the ghosts
of tomorrow.
I look at the telephone and
thank it for not
ringing.
my life has been lived
in vain;
I should have been a
shortstop, a race car driver,
a matador.
I sit in this room, I wait in this
room.
I rub my left hand over my
face.
my whiskers are sharp,
they feel good.
I think tomorrow I'll get
dressed, go outside,
I'll go to Thrifty's,
buy a roll of Scotch tape,

a bag of orange slices,
a flashlight and a
pocket comb.
then I'll snap out of it,
maybe.

d.n.f.

they shot the horse.
he kicked 4 times
with the bullet in his
brain.
his skin shone.
his skin sweated.

they pushed him into a green trailer
pulled by a yellow tractor
driven by a man in a grey
felt hat.

I walked back inside
and looked up the legs of a young woman
sitting and
reading the *Racing Form*.

she made me hot.

the dead horse had been my last
bet.

my handicapping was gone sour.

then she saw me looking.

I turned around,
walked away.

walked to a white water fountain,
bent and drank.

reading little poems in little magazines

you get so sick finally of the personal,
the relaxed and little personal
things like a visit to mother
or getting your car stolen
or masturbating in a mortuary.
the personal, the personal things:
like how big your breasts are
or how you used to be a go-go
dancer;
or how you worked the night shift
at your machine and got
slivers of hot metal under your
fingernails.
personal, personal things:
like how many wives or husbands
you've had;
or how your students ask
questions and you answer them
wrong and only realize that two weeks
later;
or how your boyfriend screwed you from
behind as you raced his motorcycle;
or how she gave you a blow job at
midnight as you drove her car
somewhere through the Arizona desert.

the personal would be all right if it was
better told
but all these little poems
are just like listening to
somebody blowing wind your way
from the next
barstool.

which reminds me:
there was this night when I was sitting
in a bar and . . .

how to get away?

things have never been
good
and they don't intend to
get better,
and the curious thing
is
that the same horrors that
plagued you in childhood
continue
in different ways,
with different faces
that speak
with the same
voice, the same
complaints, the same
hatreds,
the same cruel
demands:
how easily these faces
grow angry
over the slightest
triviality
and how
joyless, how
consistently, grimly,
joyless these faces
are, it's as if your father
or some implacable enemy
had come back now
with another
face, now more
vengeful
than ever.

must we go to the grave
having been
forever followed
by vengeful
faces?

the difficulty of breathing

                    small
                    unnerving occurrences
                    keep
                    coming up
                    one
                    after the other:
                    haphazard
                    dumb
                    accidents of
                    freakish
                    chance—
                    the tiring tasks
                    that are part
                    of our routine
                    and the
                    sundry other
                    ever-recurring
                    annoyances—
                    all these
                    inevitable
                    small defeats
                    and sorrows
                    rub and push
                    continually
                    up against
                    the
                    moments
                    the days
                    the years
                    until
                    one almost
                    wishes
                    almost

begs for
a larger
more meaningful
destiny.

I can
almost understand
why
people
leap
from
bridges.

I even
understand
in part those
people who
arm themselves
and
slaughter their
friends and innocent
strangers.

I am
not exactly
in sympathy
with them
and I decry
their reckless behavior
but I can
understand
the
ultimate

undeniable
persistent
force of
their
misery.

the horrific violent
failure
of any one
of us
to live properly
says to me that
we are all equally
guilty
for every human
crime.
there are
no
innocents.

and if there is
no
hell,
those who coldly
judge these
unfortunates
will
create
one for us
all.

help wanted and received

I'm stale sitting here
at this typewriter, the door open on my
little balcony when suddenly there is a roar in the sky,
Bruckner shouts back from
the radio and then the rain comes down glorious and violent,
and I realize that
it's good that the world can explode this way
because now
I am renewed, listening and watching as
droplets of rain splash on my wristwatch.
the torrent of rain clears my brain and my
spirit
as
a long line of blue lightning splits
the night sky.
I smile inside, remembering that
someone once said, "I'd rather be lucky than good," and I quickly
think, "I'd rather be lucky *and* good"
as tonight
as Bruckner sets the tone
as the hard rain continues to fall
as another blue streak of lightning
explodes in the sky
I'm grateful that for the moment I'm
both.

heart in the cage

frenzy in the marketplace.
cities burn.
the world shakes and calls for
democracy.
democracy doesn't work.
Christianity doesn't work.
nor Atheism.
nothing works but the gun
and the man on
top.
the centuries change and
Man remains the
same.
love buckles and dissolves:
hatred is the only
reality
on continents and in
rooms of two
people.
nothing works but the gun
and the man on
top.
all else is
meaningless.

frenzy in the marketplace.
cities burn
to be rebuilt to
burn again.

democracy doesn't work.
Christianity doesn't work.
nor Atheism.

it's just the gun,
the gun and the man on
top.

places to die and places to hide

not a chance.
nothing.
put your shoes on,
take them off.
ride a bicycle through a park in Paris.
read the great works of our time.
nothing.
watch the trapeze artist fall to his death.
no chance.
blink your eyes, scratch your nose.
nothing.
sit in the dentist's chair and stare into the face of God.
nothing.
watch the 6 horse break from the gate like a cannonball.
no chance,
the 8 horse has its number.
no chance in Vegas.
no chance in Monte Carlo.
no chance here in Southern California.
no hope at the North Pole.
put your shoes on,
take them off.
nothing.
the windows shine in the black morning
a Chinese Jew shivers in the frost.
I bury my father in a green cloak.
no chance.
I can't endure the odds but I must.
it's inbred,
I'm stuck.
there are my shoes under the bed.
look at them.
cold, dead with laces.

no chance.
the sadness roars, leaps at the walls.
one of my cats stares at something unseen.
I smile, nod.
nothing.
nothing new.
I rip the cellophane off my cigar.
nothing happens.
all of civilization collapses like a mighty wave.
a moth tentatively enters the room.
the music stops.

poem for the young and tough

yes, it's true—I'm mellowing.
in the old days
to cross my room you'd have to
step around and between
discarded trash and empty
bottles but
now the trash is
packed neatly into
sturdy garbage cans;
also I'm a good citizen, I save
my bottles for the city of Los
Angeles to
recycle
and I haven't been in a drunk
tank for a good ten
years.
boring, isn't it?
but not for me as I now
stay in at night,
listen to
Mahler and watch the walls
dance;
as a newly mellow recluse that's good enough
for me.

so I'm turning the streets back over
to you,
tough guy.

ow

whenever I see a photo of myself
I think,
Jesus Christ, look at that ugly
bloated
whale of a fish!

no wonder I had such a problem
getting them
from the couch to the
bedroom

and had to get
myself
drunk
before attempting
it.

my doom smiles at me—

there's no other way:
8 or ten poems a
night.
in the sink
behind me are dishes
that haven't been
washed in 2
weeks.
the sheets need
changing
and the bed is
unmade.
half the lights are
burned-out here.
it gets darker
and darker
(I have replacement
bulbs but can't get them
out of their cardboard
wrapper.) Despite my
dirty shorts in the
bathtub
and the rest of my dirty
laundry on the
bedroom floor,
they haven't
come for me yet
with their badges and
their rules and their
numb ears. oh, them
and their caprice!
like the fox
I run with the hunted and

if I'm not the happiest
man on earth I'm surely the
luckiest man
alive.

hey, Kafka!

tonight,
in this very dark
night,
looking out the window
at the lights in the
harbor,
there's very little to
think about or
do.

I smile, looking at
my hands—
I always had small
hands.

now
day by day
they seem to be
growing
larger.

is it some type of terrible
disease?

alone in the room
I laugh
loudly
at the thought of
my hands
growing so
LARGE
that they can't
fit all of me

into my
casket.

what a delightful frightening
thought!

"what's wrong with this
son of a bitch? his
hands are the size of
his body!"

then
I forget all that and
look out at the lights
again.

a strange visit

20 years ago when
I was a starving writer
a lady in a gold Cadillac
pulled up outside my humble place
got out and
knocked on the door.
she was well dressed,
smiling,
really beautiful.

she sat on my couch
and I poured her a drink
as she said,
"I am the Queen of
Rats in a woman's
body."

"you look great,"
I said

"I have come to invite you to live
with us
in Rat Kingdom.
the world is going to end
with a bang
soon and all that will be left
will be Rats and a few
roaches.
we admire you and I have come
to invite you to join us
before it's too late."

"come on," I said, "let's go
into the bedroom and talk it
over."

"you're being frivolous," she
said. "I'm asking you seriously if you will
join our Kingdom of
Rats.
will you?"

"have another drink," I
replied, "and I'll think it
over."

she got up then, walked to the
door, opened it, walked out.
I stood at the window,
watched her get into her
gold Cadillac and drive
off.

20 years ago
I thought it was someone's
idea of a feeble
joke.
now, I am no longer so
sure.

sometimes I think I should have
left with her.

other times
I am sure that I
did.

1970 blues

what I need, what I really need is
a blue dog with green eyes or
a fish that smiles like the Mona Lisa.

what I need, what I really need is
to never ever hear the Blue Danube Waltz
again
or to have to watch a baseball game on tv
like a slow chess match moving toward death.

what I need, what I really need is
to dream the decent dream
and I don't mean the church or god
I mean just looking up some day
and seeing one human face midst
the billions of strangled dying sun
flowers.

what I really need, what I really need is
to laugh the way I used to laugh
because in this cage
there is nothing to do
nowhere to go.

what I need, what I really need is
to confront the walls
and to get ready for that motherfucker
Death
almost with a sense of
glee.

why?: because I would be
getting away from
you.

who?

you: rat with eyes like a
  woman.

snow white

now continues
the slow retreat, still tabulating the wounds, the
escapes, the mutilated years.

there was always something in the way, something wrong,
there was never
enough.

now continues
the slow retreat,
packing age as an extra, no peace, even now.

you pluck a hair and find it to be white as
snow.

the slow retreat, no trumpets here, backing into it,
you can only wonder, did you put up a good fight?

or was it all just
a stupid joke?

we can only hope not.

now continues
the slow retreat, backing into it, going back until
finally
you reach the beginning
and can no longer be
found.

sour grapes

it's over for me, he said, I've lost it.
maybe you never had it, I said.
oh, I had it, he said.
how did you know you had it?
one knows, he said, that's all.
well *I* never had it, I told him.
that's too fucking bad, he said.
what is? I asked.
too fucking bad you never had
it, he answered.
I don't feel bad that I never had
it, I said.
I understand, he said, now go
away and leave me alone.
suit yourself, I said, and slid one
barstool down.
he just sat there staring into his
drink.
I don't know what he had lost but if
I never had it and he had lost it,
then it seemed we were in the same
boat.
I decided
some people make too damned
much of everything and
I finished my drink and walked
out of there.

fencing with the shadows

really feeling old sometimes,
pushing to get off of the couch,
puffing as I tie my shoes.
no, not me,
Jesus, please not me!
don't
put me in a fucking walker next,
plodding along.
somehow, I couldn't abide
that.
I light a cigar,
feel better.
at least I can still make it to the track
every day they're running, slam
my bets in.
keeps the heart warm and the
brain hustling.
I still drive the side streets
in the meanest parts of
town,
gliding down back alleys, peering
around,
always curious.
I'm still crazy,
I'm all right,
and I'm in and out of the doctor's
office, for this, for that, joking with
the nurses.
give me a few pills and I'm all
right.
got a refrigerator up here
in my writing room
stocked with cold ones.

the fight is still on.
I may be backed into a corner but I'm
snarling in the dark.
what's left?
the redemption and the glory.
the last march of summer.
try to put me in a walker now and I'll
kick your ass!
meanwhile, here's another cold one,
and another.
it will be a while before I
see you at the finish line,
sucker.

a hell of a duet

we were always broke, rescuing the Sunday papers out of
Monday trashcans (along with the refundable soft drink bottles).
we were always being evicted from our old place
but in each new apartment we would begin a new existence,
always dramatically behind in the rent, the radio
playing bravely in the torn sunlight, we lived like millionaires, as if
our lives were blessed, and I loved her high-heeled shoes and her sexy
dresses, and also how she laughed at me
sitting in my torn undershirt decorated with
cigarette holes: we were some team, Jane and I, we sparkled through
the tragedy of our poverty as if it was a joke, as if it
didn't matter—and it didn't—we had it by the throat and we were
laughing it to death.

it was said afterwards that
never had been heard such wild singing, such joyful singing of
old songs
and never
such screaming and cursing—
breaking of glass—
madness—
barricaded against the landlord and the police (old pros, we were) to
awake in the morning with the couch, chairs and dresser pushed up
          against the
door.

upon awakening
I always said, "ladies first . . ."

and Jane would run to the bathroom for some minutes and then
I'd have my turn and

then, back in our bed, both of us breathing quietly, we'd wonder
          what

disaster the new day would bring, feeling trapped, slain, stupid,
desperate, feeling that we had used up the last of our luck, certain we
       were finally
out of good fortune.

it can get deep-rooted sad when your back is up against the wall first
thing each morning but we always managed to work our way past all
that.

usually after 10 or 15 minutes Jane would say,
"shit!" and I would say,
"yeah!"

and then, penniless and without hope we'd figure out a way to
continue, and then somehow we would.

love has her many strange ways.

the dogs

the dogs walk quickly down the sidewalk
in the sun and in the
rain and in the dark and in the
afternoon
the dogs quickly walk down the sidewalk and they know something
but they won't tell us
what it is.

no
they aren't going to tell us
no no no
they aren't going to tell us
as
the dogs walk quickly down the sidewalk.

it's all there to be seen

in the sun and the rain and in the dark

the dogs walking quickly down the sidewalk

watch them watch them watch them
with the eye and with the heart

as the dogs walk quickly down the sidewalk

knowing something we will never comprehend.

part 3.

death will come on padded feet
carrying roses in its mouth.

cold summer

not as bad as it could be
but bad enough: in and out
of the hospital, in and out of
the doctor's office, hanging
by a thread: "you're in
remission, no, wait, 2 new
cells here, and your
platelets are way down.
have you been drinking?
we'll probably have to take
another bone marrow test
tomorrow."

the doctor is busy, the
waiting room in the cancer
ward is crowded.

the nurses are pleasant, they
joke with me.
I think that's nice, joking while in the
valley of the
shadow of death.
my wife is with me.
I am sorry for my wife, I am
sorry for all the
wives.

then we are down in the
parking lot.
she drives sometimes.
I drive sometimes.
I drive now.
it's been a cold summer.

"maybe you should take a
little swim when we get home,"
says my
wife.

it's a warmer day than
usual.

"sure," I say and pull out of
the parking lot.

she's a brave woman, she
acts like everything is
as usual.
but now I've got to pay for all
those profligate years;
there were so many of
them.
the bill has come due
and they'll accept only
one final
payment.

I might as well take a
swim.

crime does pay

the rooms at the hospital went for
$550 a day.
that was for the room alone.
the amazing thing, though, was that
in some of the rooms
prisoners were
lodged.
I saw them chained to their beds,
usually by an
ankle.
$550 a day, plus meals,
now that's luxury
living—plus first-rate medical attention
and two guards
on watch.
and here I was with my cancer,
walking down the halls in my
robe
thinking, if I live through this
it will take me years to
pay off the hospital
while the prisoners won't owe
a damned
thing.
not that I didn't have some
sympathy for those fellows
but when you consider that
when something like a bullet
in one of your buttocks
gets you all that free attention,
medical and otherwise,
plus no billing later
from the hospital business

office, maybe I had chosen
the wrong
occupation?

throwing my weight around

at 5:30 a.m. I was
awakened by this hard sound,
heavy and hard, rolling on the linoleum
floor.
the door opened and something entered the
room which was still
dark.
it looked like a large cross but
it was only a beam scale.
"gotta weigh you," said the nurse.
she was a big black woman,
kindly but determined.
"now?" I asked.
"yes, honey, come on, get on the
scale."
I got off the bed and made my way over
there.
I got on.
I had trouble with my balance.
I was ill, weak.
she moved the weights back and
forth trying to get a
read.
"let's see . . . let's see . . . hmmm . . ."
I was about to fall off when
she finally said, "185."

the next morning it was a male
nurse, a good fellow, a bit on the
plump side.
he rolled in and I stepped on the
scale.
he had a problem too, sliding the weights

back and forth, trying to get a
read.
"I can hardly stand," I said.
"just a little longer," he said.
I was about to topple off when he
said, "184."

I went back to bed and
awaited the scheduled 6 a.m. daily
blood withdrawal.

something has to be
done, I thought.
I'm going to fall off of that
scale some morning and crack
my head open.

so at midday I got into
a conversation with the head nurse
who listened to my problem.

"well, all right," she said, "we
won't weigh you every
morning, we'll only weigh you
3 times a week, Monday,
Wednesday and
Saturday."

I thanked her.

"I'll write an order on your
chart," she said.

I don't know what she wrote
on my chart

but they never weighed me
again
Monday, Wednesday,
Saturday
or any other day and I was there
in that hospital
for another two
months.

in fact, I never heard the hard sound
of that scale rolling down the hallway
again.
I think they stopped weighing
everybody
except maybe themselves
now and then.

Christ, the damned thing was
just too difficult to operate
anyhow.

they rolled the bed out of there

the nurse was standing with her back to me,
saying, "I've got to get the air bubbles out of
the line."
I began to cough and I coughed some more,
then I began to tremble, tremble and
shake and jump.
I couldn't breathe, my face was burning
but the worst was my back, right down at the
end of the spine—the pain was black and
unendurable
and the next thing I knew was
the sound of loud buzzers
and they were rolling the bed out
of there, there were 5 or 6 female nurses,
there was an oxygen tank and then I was
breathing again, the tubes stuck in my
nostrils.

they rolled me down to a large room
across from the nurses' station and it was
like in a movie, I was hooked up to a
machine that had little blue lines
dancing across the screen.

"do you still need oxygen?" one of
the nurses asked.

"let's try it without."

it was all right then.

"how much is this room costing me?"
I asked.

"don't worry, we're not charging
anything extra."

after a while they came in with a
portable machine and x-rayed
me.

"how long am I going to be in this
room?"

"overnight or until somebody needs
it more than you do."

then my wife was there.

"my god, I went to your room
and it was empty, bed and all!
why are you here?"

"they haven't figured it out yet."

"there must be a reason."

"sure."

well, I wasn't dead and my wife
sat and watched the little lines
dance on the screen
and I watched the nurses
answering the phones and
reading things on clipboards
and actually it was rather
pleasant and almost

interesting, although there was
no tv in the room and I was
going to miss the Sumo tourna-
ment on channel
18.

the next day the doctors said
they had no idea what had
caused the whole thing
and the nurses took my bed
and rolled me back to my
old room with the tiny window,
my trusty
urinal, and the little Christ
they had nailed to the wall
after my 3rd day
there.

crawl

the streets melt, I do not
smile often, I hold up these trembling white
walls.
the finish line beckons
while
the stables are full of fresh, young
runners.
the crowd screams for more action
as I don my green
bathrobe,
x-tough guy
dangling at the end of the
dream.

anything to say to the world,
sir?
no.
would you do it all over again?
no.
have you learned anything
from this experience?
no.
any advice for the young
poets?
learn to say "no."

I really know nothing at all.
the hospital spins like a top,
spewing nurses throughout the
building.
I have escaped twice before
and now is the third
time.

slow death is pure
death, you can taste a little bit of it
each day.

I am amazed that other people
remain alive and healthy:
doing their duties,
bored and/or beastly.
they swarm about,
fill the streets and buildings.
these are the fortunate
unfortunates.

I stretch out upon the bed.
my poor wife, she must live with
this.
she is a strong, good
woman.

"you're going to be fine,"
she says.

and so are:
the blue whale, the sleepy young
doctors practicing their vascular
and bariatric surgery, the simple
dark tone of
midnight.

I'll see them all later in the forest along with the
giant
gorilla.

nothing here

so much of my early life I was worried about paying
the rent, now something else is trying to move
me out of here, permanently,
and this landlord will accept no
excuses such as
"I'll pay you next week for sure!"
notice has been served on me
and my final eviction looms.
but as in the old days, I continue,
go through the motions,
read the newspaper, stare at the walls
and wonder, wonder
how did it ever come to this,
this senselessness staring me down.
all my books don't help.
my poems don't help either.
nothing or nobody helps.
it's just me alone, waiting, breathing,
pondering.
there's nothing even to be brave about.
there's nothing here at all.

my last winter

I see this final storm as nothing very serious in the sight of
the world;
there are so many more important things to worry about and to
consider.

I see this final storm as nothing very special in the sight of
the world
and it shouldn't be thought of as special.
other storms have been much greater, more dramatic.
I see this final storm approaching and calmly
my mind waits.

I see this final storm as nothing very serious in the sight of
the world.
the world and I have seldom agreed on most
matters but
now we can agree.
so bring it on, bring on this final storm.
I have patiently waited for too long now.

first poem back

64 days and nights in that
place, chemotherapy,
antibiotics, blood running into
the catheter.
leukemia.
who, me?
at age 72 I had this foolish thought that
I'd just die peacefully in my sleep
but
the gods want it their way.
I sit at this machine, shattered,
half alive,
still seeking the Muse,
but I am back for the moment only;
while nothing seems the same.
I am not reborn, only
chasing
a few more days, a few more nights,
like
this
one.

a summation

more wasted days,
gored days,
evaporated days.

more squandered days,
days pissed away,
days slapped around,
mutilated.

the problem is
that the days add up
to a life,
my life.

I sit here
73 years old
knowing I have been badly
fooled,
picking at my teeth
with a toothpick
which
breaks.

dying should come easy:
like a freight train you
don't hear when
your back is
turned.

walking papers

Dear Sir or Madam:
we must inform you that there is no room
left here for you now
and you must leave
despite all your years of faithful service
and the courage you showed on many
occasions,
and despite the fact that many of your fondest dreams
have yet to be realized.
still, you were better than most,
you accepted adversity without complaint,
you drove an automobile carefully,
you served your country and your employers well,
your compassion for
your unloving spouse and
care less children
never wavered,
you never farted in public,
you refused to exhibit rancor,
you were acceptably normal, fairly understanding and rarely
foolish,
you also remembered all birthdays, holidays and special
occasions,
you drank but never to excess,
you seldom cursed,
you lived within all the rules you never made,
you were healthy without effort,
courteous without being prompted,
you even read the classics at an early age,
you were not what we would call selfish or debased,
you were even likeable most of the time,
but now—bang!—
you're dead, you're dead, and

you must leave because
there is
no room
left here
for
you
now.

alone in this room

I am alone in this room as the world
washes over me.
I sit and wait and wonder.
I have a terrible taste in my mouth
as I sit and wait in this room.
I can no longer see the walls.
everything has changed into something else.
I cannot joke about this,
I cannot explain this as
the world washes over me.
I don't care if you believe me because
I've lost all interest in that too.
I am in a place where I have never been before.
I am alone in a different place that
does not include other faces,
other human beings.
it is happening to me now
in a space within a space as
I sit and wait alone in this room.

farewell, farewell

the blade cuts down and through,
pulls out, enters again, twists.
this is the test so
spit it out, sucker, you've long ago
demonstrated your valor
in the face of this unhappy world, in the
face of this
bitterly unhappy world,
and who but a fool would want to
linger?
your little supply of good luck has been
used up so
spit it out, sucker:
the last goodbye is always the
sweetest.

about the mail lately

I keep getting letters, more and more of
them wondering if I am really dead, they have
heard that I am dead.
well, I suppose that it's my age and all
the drinking that I have done, still
do.
I should be dead.
I will be dead.
and I have never been too interested in
living, it has been hard work, slave
labor, still is.

I've been doing some thinking about
death of late and have come up with
one disturbing thought:
that death could be hard work too,
that maybe it's another kind of trap.
it probably is.

meanwhile, like everybody else,
I do the things I do and I wait around.

I could use this poem as a reply letter
and mail out copies to those who write
me because they've heard that I am dead.
I will sign them to
give them legitimacy so that
the receivers can sell them to
collectors who can then resell them for
an even higher price to each other.

which reminds me that I no longer
receive letters from young ladies who

include nude photos and tell me that
they would love to come around and do
housework and lick my stamps.

they probably hope that I can't get it up
any more.

in any event,
I'll just continue to answer the death letters,
have another drink, smoke these
Jamaican cigars and hustle for my
rightful place in Classic American Literature
before I
stiffen up
kick the bucket
swallow the 8 ball
send up my last rocket
hustle into the dark
get the hell out
hang it up
and say my last goodbye while
clutching my
last uncashed
ticket.

life on the half shell

the obvious is going to kill us,
the obvious is killing us.
our luck is used up.

as always, we regroup
and wait.

we haven't forgotten how to
fight
but the long battle has made us
weary.

the obvious is going to kill us,
we are engulfed by the
obvious.

we allowed it.
we deserve it.

a hand moves in the
sky.
a freight train passes in the night.
the fences are broken.
the heart sits alone.

the obvious is going to kill us.
we wait, dreamless.

the hardest

birthday for me was my 30th.
I didn't want anybody to know.
I'd been sitting in the same bar
night and day
and I thought, how long am I going
to be
able to keep up this
bluff?
when am I going to give it up and
start acting like everybody
else?
I ordered another drink and
thought about it
and then the answer came to
me:
when you're dead, baby, when
you're dead like the rest of
them.

a terrible need

some people simply need to
be unhappy, they'll scrounge it out
of any given situation
taking every opportunity
to point out
every simple error
or oversight
and then become
hateful
dissatisfied
vengeful.

don't they realize that
there's so little
time
for each of us
in this strange
life to make things
whole?
and to squander
our lives living
like that
is nearly
unforgiveable?

and that
there's never
ever
any way
then
to recover
all that which will be
thus lost
forever?

body slam

Andre the Giant dead in his Paris
hotel room.
7 feet and 550 pounds, dead.

he used to wrestle.
he was a champion.

a week earlier he had attended
his father's funeral.

Andre had been a kind soul who
liked to send flowers to people.

but dead he was a problem.
they had to carry him out of
there
and no casket would hold him.

now maybe he'd get some
flowers?

Andre the Giant
in Paris
wrestling with the Angel of
Death.

and the fix wasn't in,
this
time.

the gods are good

the poems keep getting better and
better
and I keep winning at the race
track
and even when the bad moments
arrive
I handle them
better.

it's as if there was a rocket
inside of me
getting ready to shoot out of
the top of my
head
and when it does
what's left behind I
won't regret.

the sound of typewriters

we were both starving writers, Hatcher and I;
he lived on the 2ⁿᵈ floor of the apartment
house, right below me, and a young lady,
Cissy, she lived on the first floor. she had just
a fair mind but a great body and flowing blond hair and
if you could ignore her unkind city face
she was most of anyone's good dream; anyhow,
I suppose the sound of the typewriters
ignited her curiosity or stirred
something in her—she knocked at my door one
day, we shared some wine and then she nodded
at the bed and that was that.

she knocked at my door, sporadically, after
that
but then sometimes I heard her knocking on
Hatcher's door
and as I listened from above to their voices, the laughter,
I had trouble typing, especially after it
became silent down there.
to keep myself typing, as if I was unconcerned,
I copied items from the daily
newspaper.

Hatcher and I used to discuss Cissy.
"you in love with her?" he'd ask.
"fuck *no*! how about you?"
"no *way*!" he'd answer. "look, if you're
in love with her, I'll tell her not to
come around my place
anymore."
"hey, baby, I'll do the same for you,"
I said.
"forget it," he'd respond.

I don't know who got the most visits, I
think it was just about
even
but we each realized after a while
that Cissy liked to knock
while the typewriter was working
so both Hatcher and I did a great deal of extra
typing.

Hatcher got lucky with his writing first
so he moved out of that dive and
Cissy went with him; they moved
into his new apartment
together.

after that I began getting phone calls
from Hatcher:
"Jesus, that whore has no class! she's *never*
home!"

"are you in love with her?"

"hell no, man, you think I'd get hooked
on trash like her?"

Cissy would be listening on the extension
and then she'd give Hatcher an explicit verbal
retort.

after a while Cissy moved out of Hatcher's
place;
she still came around to see me occasionally
but she was always with some different
guy, all of them

real low-life
subnormals.

I couldn't understand the why of those visits;
but no matter—I had somehow lost all
interest.

then I too got a little lucky and
was able to move from the
slums; I left the ex-landlord my
new phone number
in case of
emergency.

some time went by, then the ex-landlord
phoned: "there's a woman been coming
by. her name is
Cissy.
she wants your new phone number and
address, she's very
insistent.
should I give it to
her?"

"no, please don't."

"man, she's a *number*! you mind if I
date her?"

"not at all, help
yourself."

it's strange how things like that
are good and interesting

for a while
and it's o.k. when they end and
you can simply walk
away.
but the good parts were
great and I'll
also always remember Cissy downstairs
there at Hatcher's
and me up there madly
typing
weather reports,
political columns
and
obituaries—
I wore out many a good ribbon and
worried myself
stupid, so
Cissy was memorable after
all
and that can't be said
about just
anybody, you
know?
or
don't
you
know?

a fight

pretty boy was tiring
his punches were wild
his arms were weary
and the old wino closed in and
it became ugly,
pretty boy dropped to his knees
and the wino had him by the
throat
banging his head against the brick
wall,
pretty boy fell over
as the wino paused
landed a swift kick
to the gential area
then turned and walked back up
the dark alley
to where we stood watching.
we parted to let him
through
and he walked past us
turned
looked back
lit a cigarette
and then moved on.

when I got back in
she was raging:
"where the hell have you been?"
pink-eyed she was
sitting up against the pillows
just her slippers on.
"stop for a *quickie*?
no wonder you haven't looked
at me for a week!"

"I saw a good fight. free.
better than anything at the
Olympic. I saw a good ass-
kicking alley fight."

"you expect me to believe
that?"

"christ, don't you ever wash
the glasses? well, we'll use
these two."

I poured two. she knocked hers
off. well, she needed it
and I needed mine.

"it was really brutal. I hate
to see such things but I can't
help watching."

"pour me another drink."

I poured two more. she needed
hers because she lived with me.
I needed mine because I worked
as a stockroom boy
for the May Co.

"you stopped for a *quickie!*"

"no, I watched a fight."

she tossed off her second drink.
she was trying to decide

whether I had had a quickie or
whether I had watched a fight.

"pour us another drink. is that
the only bottle we've got?"

I winked at her and pulled
another bottle from a paper sack.
we seldom ate. we drank
and I worked as a
stockroom boy for the May Co. and
she had a pair of the
most beautiful legs I had
ever seen.

as I poured the third drink
she got up, smiled, kicked off the
slippers and put her high heels
on.

"we need some god-damned
ice," she said as I watched
her ass wobble into the
kitchen.
then she vanished in there
and I thought about that
fight again.

Sunbeam

sometimes when you are in hell
and it is continuous
you get a bit giddy
and then when you are tired beyond being
tired
sometimes a crazy feeling gets a hold of
you.

the factory was in east L.A.
and of the 150 workers
I was one of only two white men
there.
the other had a soft job.
mine was to wrap and tape
the light fixtures
as they came off the assembly line and
as I tried
to keep pace the
sharp edges of the tape
cut through my gloves and into my
hands.
finally
the gloves had to be thrown
away
because
they were cut to shreds
and then my hands were completely exposed
each new slice like an electric
shock.

I was the big dumb white boy
and as the others
worked to keep pace

all eyes were watching to see
if I would
fall behind.

I gave up on my hands
but I didn't give up.

the pace seemed impossible
and then something snapped in my
brain and I screamed
out the name of the firm we were all slaving
for, "SUNBEAM!"

at once
everybody laughed
all the girls on the assembly line and
all the guys too although
we all still had to struggle to keep up with
the work flow.

then I yelled it
again:
"SUNBEAM!"

it was a total release for me.

then one of the girls on the
assembly line yelled back,
"SUNBEAM!"

and we all
laughed
together.

and then as we continued
to work
a new voice
would suddenly call out from
somewhere,
"SUNBEAM!"

and each time we
laughed until
we were all drunk with
laughter.

then the foreman,
Morry,
came in from the other
room.

"WHAT THE HELL'S GOING ON IN
HERE? THAT SCREAMING HAS GOT
TO STOP!"

so then, we stopped.

and as Morry turned away we saw that the
seat of his pants was jammed up in the crack of
his ass, that fool in control of
our universe!

I lasted about 4 months there
and I will always remember that day,
that joy, the madness, the mutual
magic of our
many voices

one at a time
screaming
"SUNBEAM!"

sometimes when you are in
a living hell
long enough
things like that sometimes happen
and then
you're in a kind of heaven
a heaven which might not seem to be
very much at all
to most folks
but which is good enough
especially when you can
watch someone like Morry
walk away with the seat of his pants
jammed up in the crack of his
ass.

apparitions

I thought I saw the one with long
brown hair standing by the coffee stand.
she had on dark shades.
I ducked and got on the escalator
and went down to the first
floor and mingled with the
crowd.

a few days later
I thought I saw the redhead.
it looked like her ass from behind
and when her head turned I'm
almost sure it was her
face.

I quickly changed floors,
went all the way over to the
clubhouse.

it might all be my imagination
that I saw 2 of the women
that I once thought I couldn't
live
without.

but
at least
I haven't run into
the other
5.

speed

every day on the freeway I get into a race with some
fool.
I win most of them.
but now and then I hook up with some fellow who is
totally insane
and then I
lose.

each day as I drive the freeway I think, not today, today
I am going to have an
easy pleasant
ride.

but somehow it happens and it's always on the
Pasadena Freeway
with its snake-like curves which enhance the
danger and exhilaration.

these same curves make it almost impossible for the police to
check your rate of speed
so they seldom cruise the
Pasadena Freeway.

here I am 65 years old
dueling with young boys
making reckless lane changes
charging into the tiniest gaps between moving
steel
the landscape roaring past in the
rain
sun
fog.

it takes an eye for split-second
timing

but there's only so far
any of us
can go.

it's difficult to see your own
death approaching

saw two writers sitting at a table in a café
the other day—not bad fellows really, either with
the word or the way.
it had been several years since I had last
seen them and as I walked over I noticed that they both
looked *old*—their faces sagged and one's
hair was *white*:
it would appear that the gentle art of poetry
had not treated them any better than working the
tomato fields, and oddly, when I greeted them,
they stammered and could barely respond,
they just sat there at the table like a
pair of old coots on a hot summer
afternoon.

I took my leave, went back to my table,
smiled at my wife, pleased that I hadn't
grown old like that, no,
not at all.

I enjoyed the view of the harbor as I looked out at the
brightly painted ships docked there, rising and falling
gently with the tide
and as I raised my glass to toast my eternal
youth
the voice across from me said, "Hank, you
better take it easy, in just another week
you're going to be
65."

made in the shade
(Happy New Year)

Popcorn Man, he don't give a damn,
hates his brother, beats his mother,
he don't give a damn,
Popcorn Man.

Popcorn Man, he don't have a
conscience, he don't wear a rubber,
hates his mother, beats his brother,
Popcorn Man.

Popcorn Man,
he'll wipe your ass with a frying pan,
Popcorn Man,
he'll steal your arms, burn your
meat, suck out your eyeballs as a
Popcorn treat,
Popcorn Man.

he don't give a damn,
he don't give a damn,
that Popcorn Man,
he really don't give a damn,
that Popcorn Man.

one for Wolfgang

today was Mozart's 237th birthday
as tonight the sounds from the harbor
drift in over my little
balcony.
I suck the world in through this cigar,
then blow it out.
I'm calm, I'm tired, I'm calm and
tired.
Mozart, what do you think?
why do the gods tease us as
we approach the final
darkness?
yet, who'd want to stay here
FOREVER?
a day at a time is difficult
enough.
so I guess everything is all right.
anyway, happy
237th birthday.
and many more.
I'd like to treat you to
a fine dinner tonight
but the other people
at all the other tables
wouldn't
understand.
they never
have.

night unto night

Barney, you knew right away
when they halved the
apple
that your part would contain the
worm.
you knew you'd never dream of conquistadors or
swans.
each man has his designated place and yours is at
the end of the line,
a long long line,
an almost endless line
in the worst possible weather.
you'll never be embraced by a lovely lady
and your place in the scheme of things
will go unrecorded.
there are men put on earth not to live but to die
slowly and badly or
quickly and
uselessly.
the latter are the lucky ones.
Barney, I don't know what to say.
it's the way
things work.
it's pure chance.
you were born unlucky and unloved,
tossed into a boiling cauldron.
you will be as soon
forgotten as last week's dream.
Barney, fair doesn't matter.
every heroic effort fails.

Barney, you have a billion names
and as many faces.
you're not alone.
just look
around.

notes on some poetry

to feign real emotion, yours or the world's,
is, of course, unforgivable
yet many poets
past and present
are adept at
this.
these are poets
who write what I call the
"comfortable, clever poem."
these poems are sometimes written by professors
of literature who have been on the job for too
long,
by the overly ambitious,
by young students of the game
or the like.
but I too am guilty:
last night I wrote 5 comfortable, clever
poems.
and if you aren't a professor of literature,
overly ambitious,
a young student of the game
or the like,
this can also be caused by too much
success with your writing,
or even be the result of a life gone
cozy.

to make matters worse, I mailed out
those 5 comfortable, clever poems
and I wouldn't be surprised if
3 or 4 of them were accepted for
publication.
none of this has anything to do with

real emotion and guts,
it's just word-slinging for the sake of
it
and it's done almost everywhere by
almost
everybody.

we forget what we are really about
and the more we forget this
the less we are able to write a
poem that
stands and screams and laughs on
the page.
we just become like the many writers who make
poetry magazines so dull and
unreadable and
pretentious.
we might just as well not write at all
because we've become
fakes, cheaters, poem-hustlers.

so look for us in the next issue of
Poetry: A Magazine of Verse,
look for us in the table of contents,
turn to any of our precious poems
and yawn your life
away.

the buzz

very few go there every day,
it's hard to beat the 18% take here in California.
I've not only been there every day, I've been
there every day for decades.
I've been there for so long that I know
many jocks' agents and trainers.
we talk
at the track or on the phone.
and they've been over to my place.
none of them are very good horseplayers
compared to me.

there are some other sad players out there.
they come day after day and lose and lose.
where they get their money, I don't know.
their clothing is old, dirty, ill-fitting, their shoes
run down.
they lose and lose and lose
and finally vanish
to be replaced by a host of new losers.

but I am a fixture.
I will come in the worst weather, the rain
falling in one gray sheet of water,
I will pull into the parking lot, my wipers working hard.
the attendants know me.
"another lousy fucking day, huh Hank?"

it's a bore between races, they
make you wait too long, they suck the life
out of you.
you lose 25 or 30 minutes between
races, time you'll never get back,

it's gone, it's gone, it's gone.
most races are 6 furlongs, which means
the real action lasts somewhere between
a minute and 9 or ten seconds.
but when your horse is closing on the
wire, that's a feeling hard to
compare.

people need a continual war of sorts, some action, the
buzz.
that's when
you come alive for a moment!

some get it at the track.
some get it in other ways.
many others seldom get it.

you've got to have it now and then,
you've got to.
a shot of fire!
an explosion!
after a photo finish
your horse's number going up
first
on the tote board!

it's the roar of the impossible.
it's as stunning as the opening of a flower.
and you standing there, feeling
that.

a simple kindness

every now and then
towards 3 a.m.
and well into the second
bottle
a poem will arrive
and I'll read it
and immediately attach to it
that dirty word—
immortal.

well, we all know that
in this world now
that
immortality can be a very
brief experience
or
in the long run:
non–existent.

still, it's nice to play with
dreams of
immortality
and I set the poem aside in a
special place
and
go on with the
others

—to find that poem again
in the morning
read it
and
without hesitation

tear it
up.

it
was nowhere near
immortal
then
or
now

—just a drunken piece
of
sentimental
trash.

the best thing about self-
rejection
is that it
saves that obnoxious duty
from being
somebody else's
problem.

good try, all

did I fail those fragile tulips?
I think back over my checkered past
remembering all the ladies I've known who
at the beginning of the affair
were already discouraged and un-
happy because of their miserable
previous experiences with other
men.

I was considered just another
stop along the way
and maybe I
was and maybe I wasn't.

the ladies had long been used and mis-
used
while undoubtedly adding their share of
abuse to the
mix.

they were always
chary at first
and the affairs were much like reading an
old newspaper over and over
again (the obituary or help-wanted
sections)
or it was like listening to a familiar
song
too often recalled and sung again
until the melody and words became
blurred.

their real needs were obscured by their
fears

and I always arrived too late with too
little.

yet sometimes there were moments
however brief
when kindness and laughter
came breaking
through
only to quickly dissolve into the
same inevitable dark
despair.

did I fail those fragile tulips?
I can't think of any one of those ladies
I'd rather not have known
no matter what stories they tell of me
now
as they edge again into
the lives of new-found
lovers.

proper credentials are needed to join

I keep meeting people, I am introduced to
them at various gatherings
and
either sooner or later
I am told smugly that
this lady or
that gentleman
(all of them young and fresh of face,
essentially untouched by life)
has given up drinking;
that
they all have
had a very difficult time
of late
but
NOW
(and
the NOW
is what irritates me)
all of them are pleased and proud
to have finally
overcome all that alcoholic
nonsense.

I could puke on their feeble
victory. I started drinking at the age of
eleven
after I discovered a wine cellar
in the basement of a boyhood
friend
and
since then
I have done jail time on 15 or

20 occasions,
had 4 D.U.I.'s,
have lost 20 or 30 terrible
jobs,
have been battered and left for
dead in several skid row
alleys, have been twice
hospitalized and
have experienced numberless wild and
suicidal
adventures.

I have been drinking, with
gusto, for 54 years and intend to
continue to
do so.

and now I am introduced
to these young,
blithe, slender, unscathed,
delicate creatures
who
claim to have vanquished the
dreaded evil of
drink!

what is true, of course, is
that they have never really experienced
anything—they have just
dabbled and they have just
dipped in a toe, they have only
pretended to really drink.
with them, it's like saying that

they have escaped hell-fire by blowing out
a candle.

it takes real effort
and many years to get damn good
at anything
even being a drunk,
and once more
I've never met one of these reformed young drunks
yet
who was any better for being
sober.

silly damned thing anyhow

we tried to hide it in the house so that the
neighbors wouldn't see.
it was difficult, sometimes we both had to
be gone at once and when we returned
there would be excretia and urine all
about.
it wouldn't toilet train
but it had the bluest eyes you ever
saw
and it ate everything we did
and we often watched tv together.

one evening we came home and it was
gone.
there was blood on the floor,
there was a trail of blood.
I followed it outside and into the garden
and there in the brush it was,
mutilated.
there was a sign hung about its severed
throat:
"we don't want things like this in our
neighborhood."

I walked to the garage for the shovel.
I told my wife, "don't come out here."
then I walked back with the shovel and
began digging.
I sensed
the faces watching me from behind
drawn blinds.

they had their neighborhood back,
a nice quiet neighborhood with green
lawns, plam trees, circular driveways, children,
churches, a supermarket, etc.

I dug into the earth.

moth to the flame

Dylan Thomas, of course, loved it all: the applause, the
free booze, the receptive ladies, but it was
all too much for him
and he finally wrote less than
one hundred poems—
but he could recite almost every one
of them
beautifully
from memory
and whether to recite or drink or copulate
soon became his only
concern.

sucker-punched by his own vanity
and the accolades of fools,
he pissed on the centuries
and they
pissed
back
all over
him.

7 come 11

things never get so bad
that we can't remember
that maybe they were
never so good.

we swam upstream
through all those rivers of
shit—
no use drowning
now
and
wasting all that
gallant and stupid
fight.

upstream through it all
to end up
sitting here
in front of this machine
with
cigarette dangling
and
drink at hand.

no glory more than this

doing what has to be done
in this small
room

just to stay alive and to
type these words with

no net below

3 million readers holding their breath

as I stop

reach around
and scratch my
right
ear.

put out the light

some individuals have an excessive
fear of death. they say that Tolstoy was
one such
but that he worked it out
by finding Christ.

whatever works,
works.

it's not really necessary
to tremble in the gloom among
flickering wax candles.

in general, most people don't
think too much about
death,
they are too busy fighting
day to day
for
survival.
when death comes
it's not so hard for them—
weary and worn as they are—
so they just toss it in,
leave
almost as if on a
vacation.

to go on
living is so much
harder.

most, given a choice
between eternal life or

death,
will always choose
the latter.

which proves
that
most people are
much wiser
than we
know.

foxholes

yes, I know there *should* be a
God.

I remember that
during World War II there was a
saying: "there are no atheists in
foxholes."

of course, there were, but I
suppose not very
many.

yet
the fear of death
does not always
compel everyone into accepting a blind
commonly-held
belief.

for those few atheists
in foxholes perhaps god and
the war both
held very little real
meaning

no matter what
the majority
demanded.

calm elation, 1993

sitting here looking at the small wooden gargoyle sitting on my
desk, it's a chilly night but the endless rains have stopped
and I am suspended somewhere between Nirvana
and nowhere, realizing that I've thought too much
about fate and death and not enough about something sensible,
like putting some polish on my old shoes. I need more
sleep but I have this horrible habit of sitting
up here until dawn, listening to the sirens and the other
sounds of the night; I should have been one of
those old guys sitting in a watchtower looking out
to sea.
the gargoyle, which looks something like myself, seems
to say, "you got that right, Henry."

this town is drying out, the drunks in
the bars are talking about the endless rain, about what
happened to them in the rain, they are full of
rain stories.
and now the new president is going to be
inaugurated and he's so damn young I could
be his grandfather, still, he doesn't seem a bad
chap but he's sure inherited a fucking mess.
well, we'll see about him and about me and finally
about you.

and what about you, little gargoyle, looking at me.
it's only January but you'll be surprised at
the hells and joys that await us,
how we are both going to have to
endure the bad parts and the galling but
necessary trivial things: a man can
damn near perish for failure to pay a gas
bill, get a tooth pulled or replace a leaking
valve stem on a tire.

there's so much crap to be attended to, like it
or not.
some just give it all up and go wild
in some corner;
I don't have the guts for that—yet.

ah, gargoyle, it's such a puzzle, you'd think
there'd be more flash, more lightning, more
miracle but if there is, we are going to have
to create it ourselves, me, you, others.

meanwhile, as I said, the whole town is
drying out and that's about all we can hope for
at the moment.

but we are girding up, pumping our spiritual
muscles, waiting here in the dream.
that's better than not waiting at all, that's better
than tossing it in.

"you got that right, Henry" the gargoyle seems
to say.

I get a chill, put on a large black sweater,
sit here, wiggle my toes.
there is something beautiful about this room.
sometimes it's just so perfect, being
alive,
sometimes,
especially while watching a small wooden gargoyle hold
up its oversized head and stick out its tongue while
half
laughing
now.

part 4.

why do we kill all those christmas trees just
to celebrate one birthday?

I have this new room

I have this new room where I sit alone and it's much like all
the rooms of my past—old mail and papers, candy wrappers, combs,
      magazines,
old newspapers and other accumulated trash is scattered about.
my disorder was never chosen, it just arrived and then it
stayed.

there's never enough time to get things
right—there are always breakdowns, losses, the hard mathematics of
confusion and
disarray.
we are harrangued by these trivial tasks
and then there are those other days when it becomes
impossible even to pay a gas bill, to answer threats from
the IRS or call the termite man.

I have this new room up here but my problem is the same as always: my
lifelong failure to live peacefully with either the female or the
universe, it all gets so painful, all so raw with self-
abuse, attrition, re-
morse.

I have this new room up here but I've lived in similar rooms in many
cities. now with the years shot suddenly away, I still sit as determined
      as ever,
feeling no different than I did in my youth.

the rooms always were—still are—best at night: the yellow glow of
the electric light while thinking and writing. all I've ever needed
was a simple retreat from the galling nonsense of the world.
I could always handle the worst if I was sometimes allowed
the briefest respite from the nightmare,
and the gods, so far, have allowed me
that.

I have this new room up here and I sit alone in this floating, smoky,
        crazy
space, I am content in this killing field, and my friends, the walls
embrace me anew.
my heart can't laugh but sometimes it smiles
in the yellow light: to have come this far to
sit alone
again
in this new room up here.

writing

you begin to smile
all up and down
inside
as the words jump
from your fingers
and onto the keys
and it's like a
circus dream:
you're the clown, the lion tamer,
you're the tiger,
you're yourself
as
the words leap
through hoops of fire,
do triple somersaults
from trapeze to
trapeze, then
embrace the
Elephant Man
as
the poems keep coming,
one by one
they slip to
the floor,
it's going hot and good;
the hours rush past
and then
you're finished,
move toward the bedroom,
throw yourself upon the bed

and sleep your righteous sleep
here on earth,
life perfect at last.

poetry is what happens
when nothing else
can.

human nature

it has been going on for some time.
there is this young waitress where I get my coffee
at the racetrack.
"how are you doing today?" she asks.
"winning pretty good," I reply.
"you won yesterday, didn't you?" she
asks.
"yes," I say, "and the day before."

I don't know exactly what it is but I
believe we must have incompatible
personalities. there is often a hostile
undertone to our conversations.

"you seem to be the only person
around here who keeps winning,"
she says, not looking at me,
not pleased.

"is that so?" I answer.

there is something very strange about all
this: whenever I do lose
she never seems to be
there.
perhaps it's her day off or sometimes she works
another counter?

she bets too and loses.
she always loses.
and even though we might have
incompatible personalities I am sorry for
her.
I decide the next time I see her

I will tell her that I am
losing.

so I do.
when she asks, "how are you doing?"
I say, "god, I don't understand it,
I'm losing, I can't hit anything, every horse
I bet runs last!"

"really?" she asks.
"really," I say.

it works.
she lowers her gaze
and here comes one of the largest smiles
I have ever seen, it damn near cracks
her face wide open.

I get my coffee, tip her well, walk
out to check the
toteboard.

if I died in a flaming crash on the freeway
she'd surely be happy for a
week!

I take a sip of coffee.
what's this?
she's put in a large shot of cream!
she knows I like it black!
in her excitement,
she'd forgotten.

the bitch.

and that's what I get for lying.

notations

words like wine, words like blood, words
out of the mouths of past loves dead.

words like bullets, words like bees, words for the
way the good die and the bad live on.

words like putting on a shirt.

words like flowers and words like wolves and
words like spiders and words like hungry
dogs.

words like mine
gripping the page
like fingers trying to climb
an impossible mountain.

words like a tiger raging in the
belly.

words like putting on my shoes.

words shaking the walls like fire and
earthquake.

the early days were good, the middle days
were better, now is
best.

words love me.
they have chosen me,
separated me from the
pack.

I weep like Li Po
laugh like Artaud
write like Chinaski.

Democracy

the problem, of course, isn't the Democratic System,
it's the
living parts which make up the Democratic System.
the next person you pass on the street,
multiply
him or
her by
3 or 4 or 30 or 40 million
and you will know
immediately
why things remain non-functional
for most of
us.

I wish I had a cure for the chess pieces
we call Humanity . . .

we've undergone any number of political
cures

and we all remain
foolish enough to hope
that the one on the way
NOW
will cure almost
everything.

fellow citizens,
the problem never was the Democratic
System, the problem is

you.

Kraznick

I met Kraznick in the post office
and like in any place of dull
toil and human suffering it was
the weird and the deformed
and the witless who always
buddied-up to me.
Kraznick talked continually about
how great he was. he was, apparently, great
at everything. his mind was great.
his spirit was noble. he would surely write
the great American novel
or play. he loved
Beethoven, hated fags. he was good
with his fists, he said, but what he
was really best at, greatest at, was
sex. he could handle the women!

actually, Kraznick didn't look too bad
from a distance. but I seldom saw him from
a distance, or if I did he would be
rushing toward me (he punched in an
hour later). we clerks would be
sitting on our stools sticking the
letters and here he would come:
"hey, man! I really caught some great head
today! she was a real pro! I was
sitting at Schwab's having a coffee
and a doughnut and . . ."

Kraznick would then talk to me for hours.
when I got off work my whole body would be
stiff with the pain of listening. I
could barely walk or steer my car.

I'll keep this short. I got out of
the post office. Kraznick stayed
on.

I'm not certain it was Kraznick but one day
I was at the racetrack and it looked like
him. he was leaning against a girder and
every now and then he would shudder. the
Racing Form rattled in his hands. I moved
off quickly. a guy like that could go off at
3 to 5 and still fall over the
rail.

Hungaria, Symphonia Poem #9
by Franz Liszt

yes, I know that I write many poems but it's not
because of ambition, it's more or less just something
to do
while I live out my life
and
if I have to write one hundred bad poems to get one good
one
I don't feel that I'm wasting my time
besides
I like the rattle of the typewriter, it sounds so professional
even when
nothing
is really happening.

writing is all I know how to do and
I much prefer the music of great classical
composers so
I always listen to them while I'm typing
(and when I finally write a good poem
I'm sure they have *much* to do with
it).

I am listening to a composer now who is taking me completely
out of this world and suddenly
I don't give a damn if I live or die or pay the
gas bill on time, I
just want to listen,
I feel like hugging the radio to my chest so
that I can be part of the
music, I mean,
this actually occurs to me and I wish I could capture
what I am hearing

and write it
into this poem
now
but I can't,
all I can do is sit and listen and type small
words as he makes his grand
immortal
statement.

now the music is finished and I stare
at my hands
and the typewriter is
silent
and suddenly I feel both
much better
and far
worse.

Club Hell, 1942

the next bottle was all that
mattered.
to hell with food, to hell with
the rent
the next bottle solved
everything
and if you could get two or
three or four bottles ahead
then life was really good.

it got to be a habit,
a way of living.

where were we going to get that next
bottle?
it made us inventive, crafty,
daring.
sometimes we even got stupid
and took a job for 3 or 4 days
or a week.

all we wanted to do was sit
around and talk about
books and literature
and pour down the
wine.
it was the only thing that made any
sense to us.
in addition, of course,
we had our adventures:
crazy girlfriends, fights, the
desperate landladies, the
police.

we thrived on the drinking and
the madness and the
conversation.
while other people hit time
clocks
we often didn't even know
what day or week it was.

there was this small gang of us,
all very young, it changed continually
as some members just
vanished, others were drafted,
some died in the war
but new recruits always
arrived.

it was the Club from Hell
and I was Chairman of the
Board.

* * *

now I drink alone in my
quiet room on the
second floor facing the San Pedro
harbor.
am I the very last of the
last?
old ghosts float in and out of
this room.
I only half-remember their faces.
they watch me, their tongues
hanging out.
I lift my glass to them.

I pick up a cigar, stick it into
the flame of my cigarette
lighter.
I draw deeply
and there is a flare of blue
smoke as
in the harbor
a boat blasts its
horn.

it all seems a good show, as I wonder again
as I always have:
what am I doing
here?

unloading the goods

it was after
my 9-hour shift as a stock boy
wearing a green smock
and pushing my wagon full of goods
up and down the crowded aisles
listening to the complaints
of the neurotic salesgirls
and angry customers
that I returned home to our place
and she was gone
again.

I went down to the corner bar
and there she sat.
she looked up as all the men
edged away from her.

"take it easy now, Hank," said the barkeep.

I sat down next to her.
"how's it going?" I asked.

"listen," she said, "I haven't been here that
long."

"I'll have a beer," I told the
barkeep.

"I'm sorry," she said.

"for what?" I asked.
"this is a nice place. I
don't blame you for coming here."

"what is it with you?" she asked.
"please don't act crazy."

I drank my beer slowly.
then I put the glass down and walked out.

it was a perfect night.
I'd left her where I had first
found her.
even though her clothes were in my closet
and she'd be back for them
it was the end
I was making it the end.

and I went into the next bar
sat down and ordered a beer
knowing
that what I once thought would be hard
was really very easy.

I got the beer and drank it
and it tasted far better
than any beer
I had had during
the two long years since we
first met.

Saratoga hot walker

sometimes when I'm standing around feeling good
it will happen
it does happen again and again
somebody will come up to me and say,
"hey, I know you!"
they will say this with some
excitement and pleasure,
and then I'll tell them,
"no, you have me confused with
someone else,"
but they'll go on to insist
that I can't fool them:
I was a desk clerk at this vacation
resort in Florida,
or I was a hot walker at
Saratoga, or I used to run numbers in
Philly,
or they saw me play a part in some
non-descript movie.
this makes me smile.
it pleases me.
I like to be seen as a
regular old guy,
a gentle member of the race,
a good old guy still struggling
along,
but I must then explain to them that
they are wrong about who they think I am
and then I walk away
leaving them somewhat confused and
suspicious.

the strange thing is that when I'm
standing around

not feeling good
worried about trivialities
scratching at minor wrongs
nobody ever comes up to me
thinking that I am
someone else.
the mob knows more than you
suspect
about
off and
on,
dead or
alive.

we change each moment
for good or ill
as time passes
and they
(like you and me)
prefer the up times
the light in the eye
the flash of lightning
behind the mountain
because as far as is known
if despair finally comes to
stay
nobody is ever mistaken
for someone else;
so
as long as they
continue to walk up
to me
and confuse me with someone

truly alive
I can hope
that in some real sense
I must be truly living
too.

the sixties?

I don't remember
much
about the sixties
I was working
12 hours a night
in the post office

but I do remember
one day
a friend of mine
took me to his friend's
house.

it was a strange-
looking house—
they had
painted it
red yellow green
and blue.

the colors
ran in every
direction and also
ran together—
very
psychedelic.

inside there were
many people
lying around.
they didn't move
much.

they appeared to
be asleep

although
it was only
one p.m.

"these are the
beautiful people,"
my friend told
me.

"yeah," I said,
"some of the women
look
pretty good."

I was feeling
smart and walked
over to the
best looker.

she had long
blonde hair
and an
almost perfect
body.

she was
stretched out
on a couch
near the
fireplace.

I shook
her.

"come on,
baby, let's
fuck!"

"peace, brother,"
she said,
"some other
time."

we walked on
through
the house.

I asked my
friend,
"how can all
these people
sleep
with all that
loud music
playing?"

he laughed,
"you're a real
cube."

we left and
went back to
his house.

we sat and
talked
while his
wife created
ceramic art
in the
kitchen.

I slept on
their couch
that night
and left
in
the morning.

I saw
my friend
again
about
three weeks
later.

driving over
I passed
the house
where
I had seen
the blonde
on
the couch.

now the
house was painted
grey,
grey and
white.

I went
to
my friend's
house.

his wife was
in the kitchen
working
on collages.

after
a few drinks
I asked
him,
"what happened
to the house
down
the street?"

"they were
too obvious,"
he said,
"they got
busted."

"that grey
and white
paint job,"
I said,
"it's hardly
as nice."

"that's true,"
he said.

we looked at
each other.

"they should
have painted
it
grey and
blue,"
I told
him.

experience

she claimed to be
worldly
to have traveled
everywhere
was said to have known
many famous men and even
slept with some of
them.

really she had
(she said)
done it
all.

after dinner
at a neighborhood Japanese restaurant
I asked her
if she would care for a
drink.

she ran her eyes
over the menu
then said she guessed
she'd have the
sake

which I
ordered.

and when the drink
arrived
she picked it
up

sipped
then quickly set it
down

looking disgusted.

"what's the matter?"
I asked.

she replied,
"why is this
stuff
hot?"

fame at last

I turn on the landing lights and head for the
runway where the crowd waits.
what a fucking farce
but I've got to play it out.
the plane rolls to a stop.
I step down into the crowd,
mikes in face, cameras on.
I answer questions
on the run.
really can't be bothered, you know.
I shove through.
they make you feel important.
Jesus, don't they have anything else to do?
a young girl screams my name.
I give her the finger.
there, that'll hold her.
where was that whore when I was
living on boiled weenies?

I finally fight my way to the limo.
couple of babes in there.
well, what the hell.
somebody else in there.
forget his name.
he hands me a drink.
now, that's better.
I tell the driver, "get the fuck out
of here!"
we move out.

the guy who handed me the drink
says, "we got you booked on Letterman
tomorrow night."

I drain my drink.
"fuck that, I'm not going!"
"but it's national tv!"
"fuck 'em! fix me another drink!"

we are on the freeway then,
going somewhere.
my place? a hotel? I don't know.
one of the babes asks me a
stupid question.
I don't bother to answer.

everybody's stupid, it's a stupid, stupid
world.
I'm all alone.
I get the second drink, slam it down.

"stop the car!" I yell at the
chauffeur, "I want to drive!"

"but, sir, we're on the freeway!"

"stop the fucking car!"

nobody says anything,
the babes or the guy talking about
national tv.
the chauffeur works his way to
the shoulder, parks it, gets out,
opens the door.
I climb out.
"you," I tell him, "sit between the
whores!"

he does as I say.
I get in front, put it in drive and
slide into traffic.

it's been a long hard month.
I open the limo up, real power, it's
cool.

"somebody fix me another
drink!" I yell back at them.

it's been a long month, a long
one.
I've got to
unwind!

doesn't anybody else realize what it's like to
be alone at the
top?

party of nine

"Hitchcock, party of nine!"
someone shouted.
and here they came, my god,
some with zippers open, others
with their shirts hanging out,
coats flung over their shoulders,
grinning and belching, nine fellows
out for a good time!
they sat down and began
beating on the table demanding
drinks and while the pounding
was going on, one of the men
made a crude remark
to the waitress, must
have been funny for they all started
LAUGHING, a couple of them nearly falling
off their chairs.
then some of them got up,
began grabbing drinks from nearby tables
to the astonishment of
the other patrons,
gulped the drinks down,
and then one of them began a striptease;
disrobing as the others
applauded
he stripped quickly to his
red and blue shorts.
I mean, these fellows were determined to have
a GOOD TIME!
some of the other
diners began shouting at
them:
"ASSHOLES!"

"SIT DOWN AND SHUT UP!"
"GO SOME PLACE ELSE!"
but they didn't seem to hear as
their drinks arrived.
then they started yelling their
orders at the waiter:
"I'LL HAVE ROAST LAMB AND
APPLESAUCE!"
"I'LL HAVE THE GRILLED TROUT!"
"I'LL HAVE YOUR ASS ON A PLATTER!"
"I'LL HAVE . . ."

as the police suddenly arrived the fellow in
red and blue shorts rose and said,
"what's the matter, officer?
we're only having fun!
what the hell's wrong?"
"yeah," said one of the others, "what the
hell's wrong?
we're only having fun."

then the lights went out.
a woman screamed.
chairs scraped on the floor
as people began to leave their tables.
outside, sirens were approaching.

the party of nine
ran back outside to the parking lot,
jumped into their cars and gunned them to
the exits.
the police couldn't tell who was who,
who was in what car.

red and blue shorts
was one of the first out in a yellow
convertible.
the officers managed to stop a few cars, all the wrong
ones.

the restaurant, one of the very best in town, took
a huge financial and public relations hit.
it was one of those special places
in the better part of town
where the famous, the talented and the rich
preferred to dine
and where they could
on occasion
let off a little
steam.

he showed me his back

I had worked there 14 years, mostly
on the night shift, eleven-and-one-half
hours a night.

one day out at the track this fellow
walked up to me.
"hey, man," he said to me, "how are you?"
"hello," I answered.
I didn't remember him,
there had been 3 or 4 thousand of us working
together in that building.

"I wondered what happened to you,"
he went on, "did you retire?"
"no, I quit," I told him.
"you quit? then what'd you
do?"
"I wrote some books.
I got lucky."

without a further word he turned
and walked off

he thought it was bullshit.

well, maybe it was,
but at least it was my bullshit, not
his.

the unfolding

I don't know
but I think sometimes that fellows like
Ezra and Céline and Ernie, Babe Ruth, Dillinger,
DiMaggio, Joe Louis, Kennedy, LaMotta,
Graziano, Willie Pep and Roosevelt
just had a little more than the
rest of us.

or is it just ballyhoo and nostalgia
which seems to separate them from
us?

actually, there are probably others
here among us
who are better at what they do
(or at least just as good)
as our heroes of the past
but
for us now
they are too close—
we pass them in the hall
see them waiting at stop lights
or buying
Xmas trees and windshield wipers
or we see them
standing quietly in line at the
post office.

one of the few grand things
in this life
are the brave and talented people
living
among

us

unnoticed.

life has both kind
and unkind
ways.

drunk before noon

she knew Hemingway in Cuba
and she took a photo of him one day
drunk before noon—
stretched out on the floor
face puffed with drink
gut hanging out
hardly looking
macho
at all.

he heard the click of the camera,
lifted his head a bit from the
floor and
said, "honey, *please* don't ever publish that
photo!"

I have the photo framed now
on the south wall
facing the door.

the lady gifted me
this.

now her book has just been
published in Italy and is
called
Hemingway.

there are many photos:
Hemingway with the lady and her
dog.

Hemingway's work
room.

Hemingway's library with mounted water buffalo
head.

Hemingway feeding a
cat.

Hemingway's bed.

Hemingway and Mary, Venezia, 31
Ottobre 1948.

Hemingway, Venezia, Marzo
1954.

but
no photo
of Hemingway
soused before
noon.

for a man who was very good
with the word

the lady kept
hers.

thumbs up, thumbs down

"the acting was really good, wasn't
it?" she asks.
"no," I answer, "I didn't like it."
"oh?" she says.

I didn't know what else to say.
once again we have disagreed on
a performance.
this time it was on tv.

I rise from the couch.
"please let the cat in," she says.
I let the cat in.
then I walk up the stairway.

I won't see my wife again until bedtime.
I sit here, light a cigar.

I can't help it, it's difficult for me to
like much of what is being currently
written and performed.
my wife tends to blame my
childhood, a certainly restricted and
loveless
upbringing.
yet I tend to believe, that in spite of
this, I still have the ability to make good
judgments.

well, things could be worse:
earthquake, a 6-day rain, a run-
over cat.

I lean back, draw deeply on the
cigar, then let it all out:

a wondrous cloud of blue–gray
smoke
as my insufficient critical soul winks at
eternity and then
yawns.

they are after me

more and more I get letters
from young men who say they are
going to take my place, that I've had it too good
for too long, that they're going to kick my ass,
strip me of my poetic black belt, etc.

I am astonished how sure
they are of their literary talent.
I suppose they have been bolstered
by their wives, girlfriends, mothers,
teachers, barbers, uncles, brothers,
waitresses and even the gas station
attendant.
but why would they want to knock
a nice guy like me off his perch?
I listen to Mahler, tip 20 percent, give
money to bums, get up each morning
and feed 9 cats.
why can't I keep my black belt a little while
longer?

I get drunken phone calls at 3 a.m.
"you've had it, Chinaski, you've sold
out!
I'm the REAL ARTIST, you son-of-a-bitch,
and *I'm* out on the street!
I'm waiting for you outside right now, I'm
going to beat the shit out of you,
Chinaski!"

or they come to the door and if I don't
respond, the night rings with their
curses and beer cans are flung against

the window.
all these ranting, raving, would-be poets!
and me, such a nice guy,
they want my charmed ass.

I'm sure I'll be replaced some day, perhaps I already
have been replaced.
I understand how the literary game works.
I've had my fling, a long fling
and I'm old enough so that I could die in the wink of
an eye.
I shouldn't be smoking this big cigar
or drinking one beer after
the other.
has my black belt already slipped down around
my ankles?
am I ready to step aside?
patience, patience, fellows, you'll have
your day, not all, but one or two of
the best of you.

meanwhile, can't you find somebody
else to badger?
must I always be a part of your agenda?
I'm a good guy, I haven't punched anybody
in the mouth for ten years.
I even voted for the first time in my life.
I'm a responsible citizen
keep my car washed
greet my neighbors
talk to the mailman.
the owner of the neighborhood sushi bar bows to me
when I walk in.

yet the other day somebody mailed me
a letter, the pages smeared with
shit.
it seems like
every young poet wants my charmed ass!
please wait, fellows, I will accommodate you in time.
meanwhile, let me keep playing with my poem-toys,
let me continue for just a little
while longer!
thank
you.

feeling fairly good tonight

Thou shalt not fail as a writer
because the vultures are waiting in the wings ready
to swoop down and sign their
"I told you so's."

Thou shalt not fail as a writer
because the very act of writing is the best protection
from the madness of the
world.

Thou shalt not fail as a writer
because it's the finest form of self-entertainment
ever
invented.

but Thou shall be finished as a writer
upon the hour or day of your
demise

only to have thick new books of yours
appear for years afterwards compiled
from the stockpile of poems you
left behind for your
publisher.

let it be so:
these wisps of magic
wrested from the clutch
of
death.

there's a poet on every bar stool

I was with my lady
down at the beach.

she was an over-
sexed young
lady.

she was on fire
with sex.

to her
sex was
everything:
the quivering
apex
the spouting
Nirvana.

that was
fine with me
although
I sometimes
longed for
other
things
too.

like I said,
I was with my lady
down at the beach.

we had stopped at
a little park

where
the old folks were
playing
shuffleboard.

I was
tired
after nights and
nights of
action
and in addition
I had failed her
miserably
the night
before.

the lady
pointed to
the old
folks.

they all seemed
to me to be
very pale,
slow,
drained.

"there!
over there! why don't
you go join
THEM!"

well, I didn't care much
for
shuffleboard.

I took her
by the elbow and
guided her into a
restaurant
along the
promenade.

we each had a cold
drink.

then I re-ordered
two more
and went to the
men's room.

when I came out
she was engaged in a
lively chat
with a
young fellow
with a head
like
a pig.

I was not
jealous.

in fact,
I would not have
minded
at all
leaving them there alone
together

but

we had driven down
in *her*
car.

so
I walked over
and sat down
next to
her.

"hey!" she said
to me
brightly:

"this guy writes
poetry
too!"

"umm umm,"
I said,
lifted my glass
and took a
sip.

then I looked at
him
and
smiled:

"I guess we both
are in the
same game.
good luck to
you . . ."

my lady was
taken aback by my
cordiality.

but
think about
it:

have you ever
tried riding a bus
from Ocean Park to
East Hollywood?

banging up
almost every day
against the
same young female
buckboard
may finally
drive an old man
to the edge of
his grave
but

there are worse
things.

valet

I slide out of my battered
BMW
tell the valet,
"we accept but do not
offer mercy."

he laughs, "hey, hey,
I like that!"

he is a chatty
sort.
he shows me his arm:
"look, that's from a razor.
I was trying it one
night until I asked myself,
" 'why should I disfigure
a beautiful body like
mine?' "

(he's built like an
ape.)

"either way, you're
right."

"what do you
mean?"

"I mean, do it or
don't, you're
right."

he grins: "hey,
yeah! that's
true!"

we smile at one another.

"I hear you write books?"
he says.

"that's true,
sometimes."

"where can I buy your
shit?"

"here and there . . ."

there is a line of
cars building up behind
us. it is a hot stupid
Saturday.

they
begin to
honk.

"HEY, YOU GUYS, KNOCK IT
OFF!"

"THEY'RE PUTTING THEM IN THE
GATE!"

"CUT OUT THE SHIT!"

the mob never understands
exchanges of
culture.

I move toward the
clubhouse.

my valet friend gets in and
zooms off in my
battered
BMW.

yes,
almost
anything
makes a
poem.

prescience

I was always charmed by
hypochromic beldams
inchoate slatterns,
caseated mesdames,
slimy prostitutes and
piss-drinking
shrews.

but now I prefer to
live alone and watch
as my cat sits in the
window
devouring an abandoned
cigarette.

10:45 a.m.

so I get up and go to the
bathroom,
throw water
on my face,
look at that mug
so long ago abandoned by beauty; I
wince, gag, giggle.
heroically.

hero poet
        hero man
                hero friend
                        hero hero
        hero lover
                hero bather
                        hero

bullshitter.

young girls wearing nylons
and garter belts like their mothers
used to
would love watching me here, watering a
plant, putting one white egg
into a small pot of boiling water.
I walk over
put one finger on the greasy refrigerator
door, draw a horse,
put the number 9 on him as
the phone rings
                rings
                  rings
I lift it and say, "yes?"

fear bounding up and down my arms,
I don't want to see any of them,
I don't want to hear from them, they should
all vanish forever.
what I need to protect me from them are
trenches, armies, the
blessing of a little luck.

"Hank?" says the voice, "how are you
doing?"

"o.k.," I say.

the horses of Mexico

in the old days before they had Sunday
racing in California,
I'd drive down to Tijuana in my
old car
to the Agua Caliente racetrack.
little did I realize that in Mexico the
take was 25%
(it was no wonder the prices were so
short)
and you had to pay the bandits
in parking a dollar for
"protection" or else there would be
something really wrong with your car when
you came back out.
I had fair luck with the betting down
there
but the service at the food stand
was slow and lousy but since
the bar was efficient I just went to the
bar.
but I never should have driven that
old car down there;
a breakdown and I surely would have been
stranded;
I had little money, no friends, no
parents,
but the car held up, the old dear.
on my good winning days, I'd
stay over a few hours that night in one of
the local bars;
that always seemed to make the drive
back shorter.
then Sunday racing began in

California
so why drive all that way?
a horse is a horse and a jock is a jock
and a race is a race,
but I miss Agua Caliente, that long long back
stretch which gave the jocks in a fixed
race plenty of time to pull their horses
back.
and those beautiful hills behind the track!
just getting out of the U.S.A. for a
day
cured a lot of what was driving me
crazy.
now I drive 20 miles to the local track
in a new car,
sit in the clubhouse with the other safe,
fat Americans
and I'm going really crazy all over
again but this time
without a cure.

a big night

the owner of the restaurant comes to our
table and starts philosophizing
about a number
of things: the national debt,
the necessity of war,
how to recognize a fine wine,
the mystery of love, etc.
of course, he says nothing new or
exceptional and the shrimp scampi
I am eating are
tough.
he laughs after each of his wise
pronouncements.
my wife smiles.
I nod.
the owner has been up front
singing with the piano player and
a couple of drunks.
he's an old white-haired guy,
happy to be making money in the
business
but his singing is not too
good: more or less old–
fashioned, embarrassing,
sentimental,
and the shrimp are still
tough.

he'll go away eventually,
I think
and sure enough he does after
shaking my hand one more
time.

my wife looks at me and says,
"you're drunk."

not drunk enough, I think.

I look around at the
other tables and notice
that they are all
peopled by the dead.

my wife stares at a plant near
our table.

"this plant is going to die," she
says

I nod.

a man at the table next to
us waves his hand as he talks
and knocks over his glass of
wine.

he leaps up from his chair
and stands there
bent over with his
back to us
and all I can see is his big fat
butt.

enough is enough.
I wave the waiter over for
the bill.

a musical difference

I've done much listening and some
thinking
and it seems to me
that our contemporary composers
(at least those here in the U.S.A.)
are mostly university-sponsored
and comfortable
and their work lacks that
old world desperate
romanticism and
gamble.

consider the old boys
during the last 2 centuries in Europe.
it's true that many of them were
sponsored by the so-called
Nobility
but there was a whole
pack of them who
starved
went mad or
suicided—
their lives became the ultimate sacrifice to
their art—
and
pragmatically speaking
this might seem
foolish
but I feel that
it was pretty damned brave
and that
that terrible final sacrifice
can be heard

in what they left
behind.

a man tends to lie
less
when he is starving and
trembling at the edge of
madness—

that is, most of the
time.

you tell me what it means

after decades and decades of poverty
as I now approach the lip of the
grave,
suddenly I have a home, a new car, a
spa, a swimming pool, a computer.

will this destroy me?
well, something was going to destroy
me sooner or later
anyway.

the boys in the jails, the slaughterhouses,
the factories, the park benches, the
post offices, the bars
would never believe this
now.

I have a problem believing it myself.
I am no different now
than I was in the tiny rooms of
starvation and madness.
the only difference
is that I am
older
and I eat better
food,
drink better
liquor.
all the rest is
nonsense,
the luck of the
draw.

a life can change in a tenth of
a second
or sometimes it can take
70
years.

dear reader:

before I came up here to
write poems
tonight
I was downstairs with my
wife
and on tv
was the beginning of a
documentary.

the narrator said,
"after Ken Kesey wrote
his first novel
he didn't write another for
25 years."

then Mr. Kesey came on the
screen and said,
"I wanted to live my life,
not just write about it."

I left then, went upstairs
to my electric
IBM,
sat down,
slipped in a sheet of
paper and
thought about what Mr.
Kesey had said:
"I wanted to live my life,
not just write about it."

well, each person has the
right of choice

but if the choosing was
mine,
I'd rather have both:
the living and the
writing,
because I find them both

inseparable.

not much singing

I have it, looking to my left, the cars of this
night coming down the freeway toward
me, they never stop, it's a consistency
which is rather miraculous, and now a
night bird unseen in a tree outside
sings to me, he's up late and I am too.
my mother, poor thing, used to say,
"Henry, you're a night owl!"
little did she know, poor poor thing,
that I would close 3,000 bars
waiting for the cry,
"LAST CALL!"
now I drink alone on a second floor,
watching freeway headlights,
listening to crazy night birds.
I get lucky after midnight, the gods
talk to me then.
they don't say very much but they
do say enough to take some of the
edge off of the day.
the mail has been bad, dozens of
letters, most of them asserting
"I know you won't answer this but . . ."
and they're right: the answers for myself
must come first as
I have suffered and still suffer many
of the things they complain
of.
there's only one cure for life but
I don't know what it is.

now the night bird sings no more.
but I still have my freeway

headlights
and these hands
these same hands
receiving thoughts from my somewhat
damaged brain.

the pleasure of unseen
company
climbs these walls,
this night of gentle quiet and
a not very good poem
about it.

the shadows

now the territory is taken,
the sacrificial lambs have met their end,
as the shadows get ready to fall,
as history is scratched again on sallow walls,
as the bankers scurry to collect loans overdue,
as young girls paint their hungry lips,
as dogs sleep again in temporary peace,
as the oceans gobble the poisons of man,
as heaven and hell dance in the anteroom,
it all begins again:
we bake the apple,
buy the car,
mow the lawn,
pay the tax,
hang the wallpaper,
clip the nails,
listen to crickets,
blow up balloons,
drink orange juice,
forget the past,
pass the mustard,
pull down the shades,
take the pills,
check the temperature,
lace on the gloves,
the bell is ringing,
the pearl is in the oyster,
the rain falls
as the shadows get ready to fall again.

a pause before the counter attack

it's a damned drag when your
brain and your legs get
weary and you stumble
about.
time to select your tombstone,
kid?
or maybe you'll piss everybody off
and go on for another
twenty years?
(you could pick up some new
critics that way.)
but meanwhile, I believe I'll take a
late dip in my spa in the
moonlight.
it's been a great fight and, I think, a
worthy one,
so now I'll follow my belly
down the stairway and into the
yard and into the bubbling
water.
this precious thing isn't over yet, my
friend,
it could be that I'm just warming up to the
battle
with you, with me, with life, with death
itself.
I warned you long ago that I'd
always be here to disturb your fondest
dreams!
and now it's into the foaming spa as
new poems
begin to
swirl and build
within.

picture this

I have caged the world away
from me.

I am an old eagle
smoking this fine Italian cigar.

think of it:
an old eagle
smoking a fine Italian cigar!

it has become pleasant
again
to be alive.

just like you
just for a time there
I thought I wasn't going to
make
it.

9 bad boys

Céline will bat
lead-off,
Shostakovich is in the
second
spot,
Dostoevsky should hit
3rd,
Beethoven will definitely bat
clean-up,
Jeffers is in the 5th
spot,
Dreiser can hit
6th
and batting 7th
let's have
Boccaccio
and 8th the
catcher:
Hemingway.

the pitcher?
hell, give me the
fucking
ball.

one more day

the quicksilver sun of my youth is
gone
and the mad girls belong to others
as I drive my car to the wash
and watch the boys polish it to a hearty
shine.
standing there and watching
I realize that
too much time
has slipped through my hands,
many years have vanished and now
my time left here is short.

I walk to my car,
tip the gentleman a dollar,
get in,
the quicksilver sun of my youth
gone.
I drive off,
turn left
turn right.
I am going somewhere.
my hands are on the wheel.
I nervously check the rearview mirror.

I am old game now for the young
hunters.

I stop at a red light.

it's a lovely day for the
young and strong
and I have been living here now for

such a very long
time.

then the green light flashes
and I continue
on.

CHARLES BUKOWSKI is one of America's best-known contemporary writers of poetry and prose and, many would claim, its most influential and imitated poet. He was born in Andernach, Germany, to an American soldier father and a German mother in 1920, and brought to the United States at the age of three. He was raised in Los Angeles and lived there for fifty years. He published his first story in 1944 when he was twenty-four and began writing poetry at the age of thirty-five. He died in San Pedro, California, on March 9, 1994, at the age of seventy-three, shortly after completing his last novel, *Pulp* (1994).

During his lifetime he published more than forty-five books of poetry and prose, including the novels *Post Office* (1971), *Factotum* (1975), *Women* (1978), *Ham on Rye* (1982), and *Hollywood* (1989). Among his most recent books are the posthumous editions of *What Matters Most Is How Well You Walk Through the Fire: New Poems* (1999), *Open All Night: New Poems* (2000), *The Night Torn Mad with Footsteps: New Poems* (2001), and *Sifting through the madness for the Word, the line, the way: New Poems* (2003).

All of his books have now been published in translation in more than a dozen languages, and his worldwide popularity remains undiminished. In the years to come Ecco will publish additional volumes of previously uncollected poetry and prose.